A BLESSED LIFE

A BLESSED LIFE

JAMES WOOD

CONTENTS

Chapter 1
The End of Innocence — 1

Chapter 2
Our new home — 7

Chapter 3
New Beginnings — 15

Chapter 4
A Changing World — 27

Chapter 5
Love and Hate — 33

Chapter 6
Lessons of Life — 43

Chapter 7
Mistakes and Tragedy — 59

Chapter 8
Living with Loss — 69

Chapter 9
Genuine Love — 81

CHAPTER 1

THE END OF INNOCENCE

The earliest memories of my life go back many years ago when I was only a small child. I was maybe three or four years old eating a bowl of Cheerios at the kitchen table at my Grandmother Sim's house in Batesville, Arkansas. I recall how she taught me to pour coffee over a biscuit and sprinkle some sugar on top of it for a tasty treat. She also liked to dip her cornbread into a glass of milk for an afternoon snack.

My grandmother was born in 1905, and she was a wonderful woman that was full of spirit and joy. She loved to cook, crochet, and yarn for a leisurely activity. The blankets, quilts, and comforters that she made were like intricate pieces of woven art. Her baked items were often entered into the county fair where she took many blue ribbons. She would also make her own jellies and preserves along with sorghum and molasses.

She told me about God and Jesus and Heaven too. I still remember her saying to me, *"Always tell yourself, I am going to heaven. And when you die, you will go to heaven because that is what you believe."* She taught me about the Bible verse John 3:16 which said God loved the world so much that he gave his only begotten son to die for our sins, and whosoever believes shall not perish but have everlasting life.

My family was living with her while my father found us a place of our own. My mother and my three siblings lived there with me and grandmother. I was a young innocent child that thought everybody loved each other, especially relatives. I looked up to my older siblings; one brother and two sisters, with love and admiration. However, my siblings did not feel the same love for me that I felt for them.

The abuse and torment began for me around this time of my life. The mental and physical anguish would last for many more years until around my thirteenth birthday. The first memory that I can remember is when my brother was playing outside with his friends. I was playing in the yard when I began to watch them at play. They were riding bicycles in the street and pulling each other around on a skateboard with a rope tied onto the back of my brother's bike. They were taking turns riding the skateboard and it looked like fun to me.

Excitedly, I ran over to them to ask for a turn on the skateboard. My brother responded with a yes but stated that I would probably fall. He said, "*You do not know how to ride a skateboard and leave us alone, but I will let you ride it to teach you a lesson.*" He seemed aggravated and angry for some reason, but I jumped onto the skateboard and grabbed the rope anyway.

My brother began pedaling the bike and took off down the road. I could see the rope unraveling the faster he got going, and as the rope grew taut, I began rolling down the street too. I may have rolled five feet at the most, and I lost my balance and fell to the pavement. I was still laying in the street when I heard a noise approaching me from behind. I quickly turned my head to see my brother pedaling very fast right toward my face.

At the last second, he tried to "bunny hop" over my face, but his front tire did not clear me. I tried to turn away from the oncoming bicycle, but I was not fast enough. The tire ran over my mouth which busted my lip and smashed a baby tooth up into my gum.

My brother crashed the bike upon impact with my face as he

hurled to the street below. He ran over to me and yelled at me to get away from him and his friends. He did not check on me one time. I ran inside to show my mother what happened, and she gave me a whipping for bothering the older boys.

The tooth stayed jammed into my gum for so long that it caused the adult tooth to have a cavity in it by the time that my mother finally took me to the dentist. I recall the dentist telling her that if she would have brought me in sooner then the adult tooth would have been fine. My lip was permanently disfigured as well which made my lip appear to have a "fat lip" look.

Secondly, we were still living with my grandmother when my older sister was playing in the living room by the air conditioning window unit. I was curious to see what she was doing over by the window. I approached her and said, "He*y sis, what are you doing?*" She turned angrily and said, "G*et out of here and leave me alone!*" I noticed that she had a steak knife cutting on some watermelon seeds while she was warning me to leave her alone.

Before I could turn to leave, she turned back around and saw me still standing there. At that time, she swung the knife grasping it in her hand toward my face exclaiming, "*I said get out of here!*" The knife narrowly missed my face and right eye and my nose somehow, but it cut my left eye. It did not hurt that much, but it felt like getting poked in the eye.

I cried out, "*Oh, my eye!*" in fear when I felt the pain, and my sister yelled back, "*I did not even touch you, you little twerp!*" My mother and grandmother were in the kitchen at this time, and they heard the commotion. My mother yelled from the other room, "*What is going on in there?*" I responded, "*She cut my eye with a knife!*" My sister answered back, "*He is a liar, I never touched him!*"

My mother came into the living room with us and grabbed me by the face to look at my eye. There was no apparent damage. Mother said, "*I do not see anything wrong with your eye.*" My sister said, "*I told you that he is a liar!*" So, my mother told me to go to bed with no supper for being a liar even though it was still early in the afternoon.

I lay in bed listening to the rest of my family eating dinner and talking about me being a liar. I woke up sometime in the middle of the night with my grandmother rubbing my ankle. I wanted it to be my mother, but it was not her. I raised from the bed and saw grandmother crying and patting my leg. She was saying, *"I am so sorry baby, I am so sorry."*

The next morning, I awoke to the smell of bacon and breakfast being cooked in the house. I could hear my family eating breakfast without me. I was very hungry since I did not eat any supper. My older siblings left for school, and I got up out of bed to go into the dining room where mother and grandmother were sitting at the table.

Grandmother said, *"Good morning! I bet you are starving. Sit down and I will make you a plate."* There were still eggs, bacon, sausage, biscuits, and gravy left on the table. Mother said, *"No. I will get him a bowl of cereal instead, liars do not get to eat good food."* I did not mind eating the cereal. Anything was good to me considering the fact that I had not eaten all night.

My eye was still bothering me which felt like a scratchy feeling every time that I blinked. I was rubbing my eye and eating my cereal when grandmother said, *"You know, he sure is messing with that eye a lot, maybe he is not a liar!"* Mother grabbed me by the chin and cheeks squeezing my face pulling me across the table towards her which made me spill my cereal.

Exclaiming, *"My God, I guess that I will look and see!"* After looking at my eye, she threw my head back so hard that my chair slid a little across the floor. Then she said, *"My God, I guess that I am going to have to take him to the doctor!"*

Grandmother said, *"Well, he sure is messing with his eye and it looks red. Maybe he is telling the truth."* A couple of days later my mother took me to the eye doctor.

She and I approached the receptionist window and mother told them who we were, and the lady in the window asked my mother what was the reason for the office visit. Mother stated, *"He says that his eye is hurt, but I think that he is a liar."* I could see a man wearing a white jacket standing next to the receptionist reading a file. However, my mother could not see him from where she stood.

The man wearing the white jacket overheard my mother's conversation with the receptionist. I saw him look away from the file in his hand to see who was at the window. He quickly put down the file and left the office to come around to the waiting area. The doctor came up to me and grabbed me by the wrist telling me to come with him.

He led me out of the waiting area then down the hallway in through a door into an examination room. Once inside the room, he placed me in a chair and pulled some type of eye inspecting instrument over in front of my face. He inspected my eyes with many different lenses while never saying one word to me. After sorting through many different lenses he said, *"Just what I thought!" Then,* he pushed the device away from my face.

He grabbed me by the wrist again and said, *"Come with me."* We went back down the hallway into the waiting area. I saw my mother and my siblings sitting down across the room. The doctor spoke out across the room to my mother and said, *"I will have you to know that your son is not a liar!"* My mother stood up from her chair and looked over to my older sister to say, *"You said that you were telling the truth."*

Once we left the doctor's office we got into the car and my mother said to me, *"When we get home, you are going straight to bed with no supper again! You humiliated me in front of everybody in there!"* My sister who was the liar did not receive any punishment for her actions even though my eye was cut badly enough which required two surgeries over the years, and the cut damaged my pupil which caused my eye to lose the ability to focus. Another permanent injury caused by my siblings which I got punished for by my mother.

The first surgery took place when I was in first grade. I had to wear a patch over my eye at school, and the other children laughed at me and called me pirate. I had to take my school picture wearing the patch in first grade and the next year in second grade as well. All while enduring more heckling from the other children.

CHAPTER 2

OUR NEW HOME

We finally moved into our own home shortly after the eye incident, but the abuse did not stop. My older brother and sister would beat on me daily with their fist. They would laugh and giggle like they thought it was funny. They would pinch, thump, hit, scream in my ear, twist my arm until I begged for mercy and hold me down punching all over my body from head to toe. My father knew little about the abuse because he was always at work, and my mother did nothing about it. She would usually punish me for their actions.

Another time, I was in my bedroom with the door shut. My brother and sister came into the room with an evil look in their eyes. They came over to my bed and held me down beating me with their fists and knuckles. Somehow, I broke free from them and ran out of my bedroom screaming and crying for help. I made my way into the living room where my mother was watching television.

I ran to her in need of protection telling her that they were beating on me again, but she grabbed me angrily and said, *"You are just a little tattle tale!"* She bent me over her lap and gave me ten licks all with my siblings watching and laughing, sticking their tongues out while standing in the doorway. I was only seven years old at that time.

A few days later, I was again laying in my bedroom with the door shut. I was all ready for bed wearing just my underwear when I heard my parents calling for all of us to come into the living room. They were going to my father's company Christmas party that night, and they were leaving my brother and sister in charge. Much to my surprise, my father said, *"We are going to a Christmas party, and we are leaving your brother and sister in charge."* He looked at them and said, *"Now you two are going to be good right?"* They answered, *"Yes sir, we promise."*

The second that my parents departed from the house, my nice sister bolted up the stairs. I heard her run into the bathroom locking the door behind her. My older siblings were near the bottom of the stairway, and I was standing in the living room near the bottom of the stairs. I looked towards them as they were turned looking up the stairs. They heard my sister locking herself in the bathroom.

Suddenly, they turned to look in my direction. They had that evil look in their eyes once more. I heard my parents' car outside so I ran out the door to get their attention. I barely eluded my siblings as I reached the front door. One of them grabbed my arm, but I managed to slip away from them.

However, I was too late to catch my parents. They were just pulling away as I ran out the door and they did not see me. I heard the front door slam behind me, and I heard them locking me out in the cold night. I took off running down the street trying to catch my parents, but I could not get their attention. After I had ran a block down the road, I saw them turning right onto the highway, and I knew that they were gone. At that time, I looked down at myself to notice that I was outside wearing nothing but my underwear.

I decided to make my way back home because it was cold outside and I was scared and ashamed. I did not want to go home either though. I did not know what to do. I made my way home and snuck around to the back door. I was afraid to go into the house, but I was freezing cold. So, I checked the doorknob to see if it was unlocked.

Somehow, my older siblings knew that I was at the back door.

About the same time that I reached to check the doorknob, I heard them locking it from the inside. They were yelling and cussing at me from inside the house. They said, *"I hope you freeze out there you little pussy!"* They laughed and berated me from inside the house.

I sat down on the back porch for awhile, but I started thinking that they might open the back door and grab me. So, I chose to go around to the front of the house. I waited outside for a few hours until my parents returned home from the Christmas party. Finally, they pulled into the driveway. It seemed like an eternity since they had left for the party.

My father got out of the car and said, *"What are you doing out here in your underwear?"* I answered, *"They locked me out!"* My father replied, *"That door better not be locked!"* He reached to turn the doorknob and gave it a twist, but it did not turn because it was locked. He quickly retrieved the key to the front door, but my brother and sister unlocked the door before he could find the correct key.

My father asked them, *"Why is this door locked?"* They both started stuttering about as they tried to lie to him. They told him that it was not locked, but he had already checked it for himself. My mother also witnessed that the door was locked too. We all came inside the house to the living room, and my father began to question them on why I was locked outside. Nonetheless, they denied everything about the whole night. They acted all innocent and told father that I had snuck out of the house, and they did not know where I was at.

My father realized that my other sister was not with us in the living room. He said, *"Where is my daughter?"* About that time, she came out of the bathroom. He asked her, *"Where were you?"* She replied, *"I was hiding in the bathroom. I heard them in their bedroom before you and* mother *left for the party. They were planning to hurt me and my brother. So, I ran upstairs and locked myself in the bathroom when you guys departed for the party!"*

My father then turned his attention back to me and said, *"So you ran outside?"* I said, *"Yes. They tried to grab me when I got to the door, but I got away from them."* Then my father grabbed me by the wrist and raised my arm up above my head turning me around in a circle. He said. "*My God, what is all over him? He is bruised from head to toe!*" He turned to my mother and said to her, "*I thought you said this abuse had stopped. You said that you would tell me if this was still going on!*" My mother lied to him and told him that she was unaware of the continuing abuse.

She knew of the maltreatment because a few days earlier is when she whipped me for tattling on them for beating me in my bedroom. I was so used to the abuse that I was unaware of the bruises on my body. I went into the bathroom to look at myself in the mirror and I was amazed at the numerous bruises.

My younger sister and myself were told to go to bed while mother and father dealt with my older siblings. I do not know what happened that night after I fell asleep. I woke up the next morning to find my mother sitting alone in the living room. My father had gone to work and my siblings were not downstairs. My mother angrily said to me, "*I hope your happy now! Your brother and sister had to move in with grandmother! I hope your proud of what you have done!*" I was thinking to myself, what I have done? I am the one that was bruised and abused. It should be what they have done, not what I have done!

The abuse was temporarily halted for a short time. My mother and father along with my younger sister and myself continued to live in that house until 1977. I remember it vividly because it was the same year that Elvis Presley died in Memphis, Tennessee. That same year my father accepted a new job in another town, and we moved into a different house.

I was informed by my mother that my older siblings were moving back home. My older siblings picked up right where they had left off with the abuse. It began the first day they came back home. They started punching and threatening me on a daily basis while they would hold me down and make me beg for mercy. I always feared that they wanted to kill me. They were so evil and mean which made me feel unsafe in our home.

My father had a talk with me shortly after they moved back

home. He asked me if they were still hurting me, and I told him yes they are still beating on me. He told me that he had done everything that he could do and that I was going to have to stop them myself. He told me to defend myself when they tried to hurt me again. He taught me about fighting and boxing techniques, and he told me to punch them right in the nose the next time they messed with me. He knew that they would be less likely to approach me once I stood my ground.

Not long after our discussion, I was sitting in the living room by myself watching television when my brother came along and flopped himself down on my lap. He started aggravating me rubbing my face saying, *"Look at the little pussy boy, your just a little pussy boy."* I remembered what my father had told me, and I felt a bolt of energy go through me when I balled up my fist and punched him right in the face. I was aiming for his nose, but he turned away and the punch landed on his cheek.

The impact of the punch knocked my brother to the floor, and it made a loud noise which my mother heard in the kitchen. She came running into the living room to see my brother on the floor. She said, *"What is going on in here?"* I told her that he was picking on me again, and I had to punch him to make him stop. She knew that I was watching television by myself before my brother had come into the room.

She told my brother that he should leave me alone. She told him, *"That is what you get!"* She asked me why I decided to hit him, and I told her that father had told me to defend myself. She said, *"What kind of father tells his children to punch their own siblings?"* It was the first time that my mother had actually taken my side, but I was also confused about the comment concerning the advice my father had given me on defending myself from my abusers. I thought that it was odd she had allowed them to punch on me, but I was not allowed to hit them in return.

The abuse stopped from that day forward. My father's advice was correct as standing my ground halted their bully tactics. My siblings continued to aggravate me mentally through the years, but their physical abuse was stopped with one punch. I never understood what I did wrong to deserve their animosity.

My mother woke me early that next Saturday morning as she abruptly slung the door open which startled me out of my sleep. She told me to get up and get dressed to meet her in the backyard. Once that I arrived in the backyard, she told me that I was to start mowing the yard every Saturday morning.

I asked her about my siblings since I was the youngest in the family. She told me that I was my father's son and therefore it was my duty and responsibility. I asked her about my older brother at which time she revealed to me that he had a different father. She was stuttering and flustered at that moment, and she told me, *"Just start mowing the yard and I will explain everything to you later."* I thought that my father was all of our father, but my mother revealed to me later that day that she was married to another man before marrying my father. My two older siblings came from her first marriage.

That same morning was the first time that I had mowed a yard. It was a difficult task for such a small child. Our septic tank leaked in the backyard which made the grass grow tall and thick. I could barely push the lawnmower through the overgrown yard, and the mower kept shutting off every time the grass would get clogged under the mower which caused the engine to stop running.

Our next door neighbor was in their backyard watching me struggle with the yard. She asked me, *"Where are your older siblings? Aren't you the baby? They are grown, they are teenagers."* I told her that they were still in bed asleep. She said, *"You poor thing. How come they made you mow the yard?"* I answered to her, *"I don't know."* She offered me some advice on mowing the yard before I restarted the engine to continue with my chore.

I had finished the entire backyard about the time that I began to feel weak. I was so tired that my body was shaking all over, and I stopped mowing to go inside to eat something. I walked into the kitchen to see my family sitting around the table eating breakfast. My mother had made them waffles and bacon.

She asked me what I was doing in the house and wondered if I had finished the yard. I informed her that I had finished the back-yard, but I had the shakes and needed something to eat. She told me to go back outside and finish mowing the yard. I reminded her that I was shaking all over, but she did not care about my well being. She told me to drink some water out of the outside faucet.

Thankfully, the water helped me recuperate enough that my body stopped shaking. I continued onward with my task until I had finished the entire yard. I was getting hungry as I grew weaker by the moment. I went back inside the house to tell them that I had finished mowing the yard. She instructed me to tell my father so he could go outside to approve of my completed task.

My father and I returned back outside to the yard. He said that everything looked good, but I did not mow the ditch line out by the road. He told me to mow the ditches and I would be finished. He went back inside the house as I finished mowing the ditches.

Upon completion of my task, I returned back into the house once again to find my family eating at the table for a second time. This time they were eating tuna fish sandwiches. I announced to them that I had finished mowing the yard, and I told mother that I was starving. She said, *"You are a filthy mess! Get out of my kitchen and go take a shower!"* So, I went to take a shower, but when I returned to the kitchen nobody was at the table. There was no food left out for me to eat. I searched the oven and the refrigerator before my mother came into the kitchen.

She said, *"What are you looking for?"* I replied, *"Where is my plate, did you not save me anything to eat?"* She told me that all the food was gone, and I would have to wait until supper before I could eat anything. Therefore, I went to my bedroom to lay down and rest. I did not eat anything until around six or seven o'clock that night when she had finished cooking supper.

I mowed that yard from that day forward for several more years.

My older siblings never mowed the yard one time. My best friend asked me about my chore and wondered why my older siblings did not have any chores. He informed me that in his family the older children tended to the more difficult tasks, and the baby of the family did very little with the chores. I never understood why my mother treated me so differently.

CHAPTER 3

NEW BEGINNINGS

I started a new school when we moved in 1977, and the teachers there were very old fashioned. My homeroom teacher would carry around a yardstick with her to use for disciplinary purposes. She would smack a student either on the back of the hand or the palm of the hand anytime a rule was broken. The back of the hand technique was more painful than the palm of the hand. So when she would punish one of the girls, she would instruct them to hold out their palms for the less painful punishment.

The other teachers used different methods of public humiliation such as pulling the students by their ear or cheek. I was standing in line one day returning to class after our recess. We were not allowed to speak while waiting in line or there would be consequences for breaking a rule. I made the mistake of talking one day, and a teacher came running down the line toward me.

She grabbed me by the ear to pull me out of line, and she scolded me with a verbal thrashing before sending me to the principal's office. She was a mean teacher. I thought she was going to pull my ear off. The principal gave me a paddling for being a discipline problem. Adults were tough and feisty back in those days. They often ruled with an iron fist mentality.

I met my best friend the first day of school. His desk was right next to mine in the rear of the classroom. He was the first classmate that spoke to me upon my arrival. My last school required a different notebook for each class, and I had about five or six notebooks. He said, *"What is the deal with all those notebooks?"* I said that I needed them for all of my classes. He answered, *"Not here. We only need one notebook."*

He instantly became my best friend. We would play together everyday at recess until one day he invited me to stay the night with him and his family. He made me feel safe and happy when I would stay the night with his family. They treated me with love and respect much like my Grandmother Sims. He was the kind of friend that made everyday better.

His family lived in town near the school, and I lived outside of town in a rural neighborhood. One day he approached me very excited and told me they were moving. I was sad for a moment, but then he said that they were moving right down the street from our house. Our friendship flourished more than ever after they moved into our neighborhood.

We spent everyday together riding our bicycles, fishing, playing in the creek, playing with our Hot Wheels collection and swimming in the local swimming holes. We were inseparable for many years. He was like a guardian angel sent from God to show me love and happiness. He was always kind to others. I never saw him ridicule another person or act out in anger or violence. He made the world a better place.

We started playing basketball in the fourth grade. The basketball coach at school would open the gymnasium every Saturday morning. We did not know how to play very well, but we had a wonderful time learning from the coach. We went to the gym every time the doors were open as our friendship grew stronger day by day.

We both decided to go out for the team, and we both made the final cut. Neither one of us started, but we were happy to make the team. The team provided me with the family togetherness that I had always longed for from my own family. They treated me with love and respect which gave me a sense of purpose and importance that I had always wanted to feel.

I loved spending time with my friends. We would ride our bicycles around the neighborhood carving trails in the fields and forest near our homes. We would journey into town quite often as well. Town was just a few miles down the highway, and we could make it there and back without our families even knowing that we were gone. Most times we would pick up soda pop bottles along the roadside during our trip into town. We would take them to the local grocery store to cash them in for the deposit refund.

I spent my money on candy, chips, and soda depending on how many bottles that we found. The days when we did not receive much money we would buy penny candy. My favorites were jolly ranchers, bubble gum, tootsie rolls, and chocolate footballs. A little bit of money could purchase a whole bag of goodies, but I would usually buy a candy bar, a bag of chips, and a soda on a good day.

The soda machines were unique back in those days. After inserting the money one would open a glass and metal door which enclosed the sodas to keep them cold. There would be a bottle opener on the front of the soda dispenser in order to open the refreshing treat. The sodas were in glass bottles that were dispensed through a circular opening inside the door.

While we were in town, we would often stop by the local pool hall. The pool hall was a fun, safe place that was an inexpensive activity. We would shoot pool for hours on some days while the old men that frequented the hall would stay in the back playing cards and dominoes. Eight ball, nine ball, and snooker was some of the pool games that we played. The old timers there were firm but fair. They looked out for us like father figures.

Other days, we would go swimming in various water holes near our homes or in town. We would swim in ponds, creeks, and swimming pools. One particular time, we went swimming in a pond that we had noticed from the highway. It was a hot, summer day so we jumped right into the water. We splashed about in the water gargling and spitting the water out of our mouths.

Our dogs had accompanied us that day as they were swimming as well. My dog Duke and my friend's dog Lucky started fighting with each other during our outing. They were in the middle of the pond snarling and growling as they would go underwater only to resurface face to face with their teeth gnashing against one another. We separated the dogs and swam a bit more before retreating home.

A few days later, I was riding by that same pond with my parents in their car. I noticed that a herd of cows were out in the pond wading around to cool off from the heat. I said, *"We went swimming in that pond the other day."* My parents turned to look as we drove past and they replied, *"I hope you did not swim in that pond! That is an old cow pond! They probably pee and poop in that water!"* I felt a little sick when I remembered how we had gargled and spit the water out of our mouths. Needless to say, I never went swimming in that pond again.

Duke became my dog the day that we moved into our new house in 1977. He was a stray dog that was hanging around in the yard. He picked us as his new family. Duke would go everywhere with me when I went outside. He would run up ahead of me going yard to yard running off the other dogs in the neighborhood. He was such a good dog that he would protect every member of my family. He would even wait on us if we went inside another house so he could safely guide us back home.

My friends and I wanted to go swimming at the local swimming pool one hot summer day. I left without my shoes as we took off down the road. About halfway there, I realized what a dumb decision I had made to not wear my shoes. The road was asphalt with black tar patches where the road had been repaired. The road was so hot that the asphalt and tar was like molten lava on my feet. I tried to walk in the ditch, but the ditch was full of stickers. So, I walked on the shoulder of the road which was mostly gravel that hurt my feet too.

My friends laughed at me as they told me to wear my shoes before we had departed on our journey. Thankfully, my feet survived the enduring journey to the swimming pool. We swam for hours enjoying the cool waters of the pool, but I kept thinking about the return trip home. I was dreading that hot tar road. The road was not as hot on the way home, and I made it back home. I learned a valuable lesson that day about shoes. They protect your feet from the elements.

My friends and I devised a plan to skip school one day in the fifth grade. We were to ride the bus to school then meet behind the bus parking lot before school. Our plan was to hang out all day in the forest behind the school. That forest was nicknamed the nature trial which had three different trails leading into the forest.

One friend was to bring supplies; sodas, chips, candy, and magazines for the day trip. My best friend and I rode the bus that was operated by our principal. So, he knew that we were at school. We met the third member of our party behind the buses as we waited for everybody to clear out pf the area. We snuck out of the parking lot and made our way down the road around the baseball field.

There was a trial out behind the gully in left field. We ventured deeper into the forest until we came upon a creek. We decided to set up camp there for the day. We sat around talking and eating snacks while looking at magazines. We wondered about our classmates at school, but we never considered ourselves. It felt like forever had passed when we started running low on supplies. So, we made the smart decision to make our way into town to gather more supplies at the local grocery store.

We took a different trail out of the forest which came out on the other side of the school. The store was only a few blocks from the nature trail. We stopped at the city park near the library to gather out thoughts. My best friend and I stayed at the park while our other friend headed out for the store to acquire the needed supplies.

Not long after our friend had departed from the park, my best friend and I were sitting on a concrete and rock bench talking about our plans for the rest of the day. All of a sudden my friend flung himself to the ground. He said, *"Get down, hide!"* So, I jumped down on to the ground next to him. I was laying there wondering to myself why we were hiding then I heard a woman's voice off in the distance calling for us both.

I looked over at my friend to see the look of astonishment on his face. We laid there in fear waiting and wondering what to do next. I heard the woman call out for the second time to both of us. That is when my friend said, *"Come on man. They found us."* We both stood up to see two women standing next to a car. They were my friend's grandmother and his aunt that had found us in the park.

They informed us that the whole town was looking for us and everybody was worried about our safety. They inquired about the third member of our party, and we informed them that he had gone to the store. We loaded into the car and headed towards the grocery store. We saw our friend walking down the sidewalk with bags of food in his hands. We pulled up next to him as he realized that our journey had come to an end.

They took us back to school where all of our parents were waiting for our return. They quickly scolded each one of us as they had to return back to their jobs. The principal took us inside his office where he advised us against our foolishness. We were all given three licks each with a paddle from the principal.

We were escorted to our classroom were everyone was eagerly anticipating our return. Our teacher scolded us for our actions, and she offered us some good advice as well. For our punishment, she made us write a one page essay on what we did all day which we had to read in front of the class.

Later that year, I joined the summer baseball program. It was my first year in little league. Our baseball team was a good bunch that made me feel important. We were a good team as well usually defeating our opponents by a good margin. One game in particular, I was standing on deck(next to bat)when I heard my father calling out to me from the other side of the fence.

He said to me, *"Hit a home run!"* I was thinking to myself that I just hope to get a hit. I responded to him, *"I wish."* He said, *"Look at their left fielder, how shallow he is standing."* I looked to see him standing a few feet behind the shortstop. He was almost standing in the dirt of the infield.

The umpire called me up to the plate to take me at bat. I swung at the first pitch that was thrown, and I made contact with the baseball. I dropped my bat and took off running to first base. On the way to first base, I looked to see where the ball had gone. I saw the ball flying over the left fielder's head as he never even saw the ball.

I rounded second base when I noticed the left fielder running out towards the gully. He had still not located the baseball yet. So, I made my way around third base and scored standing up for a home run. The entire team batted around that inning as I got to bat for a second time.

As I approached the plate for my second plate appearance of the inning, the other team's coach called a timeout. He made a defensive switch with the left fielder. The new left fielder was still on his way to the outfield when the pitcher from the other team started motioning for me to approach the plate. I looked back out to the left field to see the substitute was still not in position.

The pitcher was even more animated with his gesturing for me to approach the plate when I heard the umpire call out, *"Batter up!"* I stepped into the batter's box giving one last glance to left field to see that the fielder's back was turned away and still not ready. The pitcher seemed to be in a hurry as he threw me the first pitch. I made contact with the baseball again as I dropped my bat to begin my trek to first base.

I looked again as I made my way down the first base line to see the baseball flying over the left fielder's head. He still had his back turned to the action so he never saw the ball. I rounded second base and noticed the center fielder running to the ball with the left fielder looking around in confusion. I rounded third base and scored easily again for my second home run of the game. Two home runs in one inning is a rare feat on any level. The chain of events that led to those home runs were amazing.

Later that summer the baseball season had come to an end, and I was sitting at home waiting for the rain to stop. A flash flood warning had been issued for our area as the thunderstorms had forced me to stay indoors. I was so bored from the lack of any activities as I awaited for the storms to end.

I went outside to play down at the creek as soon as it stopped raining. I had a toy boat that I never got to play with except for in the bathtub. I thought it would be fun to take my boat to the creek and watch it floating down the stream. The creek was flowing very strong and fast that day. I did not understand how powerful water could be until that day. I put my boat in the water thinking that I would run ahead and regather it downstream.

The water swept my little boat away so fast that I could not recover it from the creek as I watched my favorite toy disappear into the distance. Next, I wanted to feel the power of the water so I got into the creek myself. A barb-wired fence crossed the creek so I made my way into the strong current while holding onto the fence. I could feel the raw power sweeping across my body, but I still did not respect the true strength of water.

I wanted to feel like Superman flying through the air by hanging onto the fence with my body stretching out behind me. The moment that I let my legs and feet leave the creek bed, I knew that I was in serious trouble. The powerful water nearly swept me away just like it did my little toy boat.

I struggled to regain my footing on the slick creek bed with the strong waters pushing against me. My boots kept slipping and sliding every time that I tried to get my feet underneath me again. The current was so strong that it pulled my boot off of my right foot. God was watching over me that day. Because with my boot missing, I was able to find a foothold in the creek bed. I had grown weary by this time as I was fighting the flooded creek for dear life.

I felt my big toe find an impression on the rock below the water. It was just enough for me to regain my footing. My left boot slipped a few more times as I grew weaker by the second, but I finally got both of my feet under me once again. I started pulling myself towards the fence moving my feet little by little until I finally reached the fence line.

I was exhausted by this point as I wrapped both of my arms over the fence to rest. The water was still very strongly pushing against my body while I tried to recover from the near death experience. Holding on with all of my might, I began to work my way across the fence line to the bank of the creek. I was breathing heavily and my body was shaking all over as I drew closer to the edge.

I had to stop for another short rest before lunging out of the creek onto the bank. The ground never felt better that day as I laid there gasping for air. I thought to myself that I was blessed to survive the flooded creek that day. It took me several minutes to garner enough energy to make my way home.

I made my way through the forest with one boot. My mother saw me coming from the woods into our backyard. She noticed that I was soaking wet and missing a boot. She ran out of the house exclaiming to me, *"What has happened to you? You are soaking wet! And where is your boot?"*

I told her about my experience with the flooded creek, and she could not believe what I had done. She said, *"There is a flash flood warning. You are not suppose to get in any waterways because they are very dangerous. People drown all the time in flash floods. You are lucky that you did not drown."* I thought to myself; I am not lucky, I am blessed because I know that God saved me that day in the flooded creek.

I rode my bicycle to town with my friends a few days later. We decided to stop by for a visit with my best friend's grandmother. We started racing back home when someone called out, *"The last one home is a rotten egg."* I took off ahead of the pack when I turned onto the highway home. I glanced back behind me to see if they were catching up to me. I noticed that my best friend's little brother was the closest one to me. The rest of my friends were about half way up the street.

My friend's little brother was riding his bike at a fast rate of speed as he attempted to turn onto the highway. I turned to look again when I saw him locking up the rear tire of his bicycle. He slid out of control across the highway and careened into the side of a bridge. I watched in terror as he slammed into the bridge and flipped over the edge before he disappeared from my sight.

He tried to hold on as he went over the edge by grasping and clawing the concrete with all his might. I slammed on my brakes and turned my bike around quickly as I began pedaling back down to the highway to check on him. His brother along with the rest of the bunch had still not caught up to us as I approached the bridge.

I rode up along the side of the bridge to see my friend's little brother laying below in the shallow creek. He had fallen onto a bunch of rocks, and he was laying in the water moaning and crying. I asked him, *"Are you all right? Do you need some help?"* He answered, *"I just crashed over a bridge! What do you think?"*

I got off of my bicycle and made my way down to the creek. It was a steep drop-off from the edge of the road, but I jumped right down there to help my friend. I walked into the creek as he was still laying there in the water. I was startled when I noticed that he was bleeding. He had a gash below his left eye from one of the rocks that he had landed on in the creek.

His bicycle was up on the bridge because it did not flip over the edge. So, I grabbed him to help him up out of the water. He was visibly shaken from the ordeal as we made our way up to the road. About the time that I was helping him up to the road, his brother along with the rest of the group finally arrived. His brother asked me what had happened to his little brother.

I informed him about his brother's wreck on the bridge. My best friend was angry because he was responsible for his younger sibling. He felt guilty because he did not keep an eye on his brother. A car pulled up next to us on the highway to see if we needed any help. They were an older couple that lived in our neighborhood.

They instructed us to put his brother in their backseat, and we loaded his bike into the trunk of their car. They said that they would take him home to his mother since he was hurt. They departed in the vehicle as my best friend and I followed closely behind. I had never rode a bike so fast that day.

My best friend and I could see their car pulling into his mother's driveway as we turned into our neighborhood. The rest of our friends were way behind us because we had pedaled our bikes extremely fast. We rode our bikes into the driveway as they were knocking on my best friend's front door.

My best friend's mother answered the door to see her son shaken and bleeding as we explained to her what had happened to him. She was frantic as she gathered her children into her car and departed for the hospital. He was mostly battered and bruised from the wreck, but he did receive some stitches in the gash below his left eye. I will never forget the sudden shock and fear the moment that his little brother went over the edge of that bridge. Thankfully, he was all right.

CHAPTER 4

A CHANGING WORLD

Later that year during my last year of elementary school, I was shocked to learn about the high school initiation. Our high school housed the seventh grade all the way through to the senior class. All male students that were new to the high school were subject to be initiated by the upperclassmen.

Red bellies were the preferred method that the high school upperclassmen chose to use. After hearing about this barbaric ritual, I began dreading the day that I started high school. I could not sleep at night because I would lie awake thinking about this cruel and unusual punishment. I had already suffered enough abuse at home, and I did not want to suffer more abuse at school.

The first day of high school for me was a day of fear. Everyday was a day of fear until one had received their initiation. I had an up close personal encounter the first day of high school when my older sister(the one who cut my eye)called out to me. She was standing with her friends under the "smoke tree." In those days, high school students could smoke cigarettes on campus, and most of the upper-classmen would hang around the "smoke tree."

Reluctantly, I went over to tree to talk to my sister. One of my friends told me not to go over there, but I went over there anyway. He decided to go over there with me. My sister was talking to somebody else when we approached her so we were just standing there right in the middle of all the upperclassmen.

I heard a mean sounding voice call out from within the group, *"Hey, are they seventh graders? What in the hell are they doing over here?"* My sister heard them berating us and told them to leave me alone. She said, *"He is my little brother. I called him over here. Leave him alone."* She was an upperclassman herself, and her boyfriend was the strongest guy in school.

I heard one of them tell her that they were sorry, but then I heard them ask her about my friend. They said, *"What about the other one? Is he your brother, too?"* She looked over at my friend and told them, *"No. I have never seen him."*

Suddenly, a group of four or five young men grabbed my friend and threw him to the ground with great intensity. Dirt and dust flew everywhere as my friend landed on the ground. The group jumped down on the ground to hold him down while one of them raised his shirt then slapped his belly repetitively very hard many times until his belly turned red. Hence, the red belly.

The initiation looked more like a beating instead of a red belly. I was spared that day because my sister and her boyfriend had taken up for me, but my friend was not so lucky. The upperclassmen seemed to find the abuse to be enjoyable as they all laughed and heckled my friend. A teacher passed by and witnessed the whole ordeal. He just laughed as he strolled by and said, *"Are they getting their red belly?"*

The initiation ritual was accepted and permitted by the entire high school staff including the principal. I was appalled that the administration would allow such abuse to take place on the school grounds. The rituals were basically assault and battery. My fears grew more intense knowing that the adults at school would not protect us from the older students.

My second encounter with the upperclassman was when my best friend and I were leaving the cafeteria after finishing our lunch. We chose to go through the parking lot in order to avoid the bullies. The parking lot was a gravel area where the students that drove to school parked their cars.

We had travelled about halfway across the lot when a group of four to five upperclassmen came out of nowhere and confronted both of us. They said, *"Well, well, well. Look what we have here! A couple of seventh grade pussies!"* They came after me at first saying, *'Get him! Get that little pussy!"*

They came up to me and reached out to grab a hold of me to begin their assault. They were still talking to each other saying, *"Get him, grab him!"* When all of a sudden, I heard a voice coming from behind us saying, *"Hey! Are y'all messing with my family!"* Suddenly, the group stopped in their tracks like they were frozen in time.

We all turned to see who was calling out to us. It was my sister's boyfriend standing at his truck with the door open while he was rolling a pack of cigarettes up in his shirt sleeve. They bullies said, *"He is your family?"* He responded back to them, *"That is my brother! Now leave him alone!"* They quickly apologized to him as he departed for class.

They backed away from me to turn their sights on my best friend. They grabbed him and threw him onto the hard gravel parking lot and proceeded with the red belly ritual. I felt so sorry for my friend as I stood by helplessly observing the beating. When they finished the ritual, they turned to me and said, *"We are gonna get you, you little pussy! You won't always have someone there to save you!"*

My best friend stood back up and dusted himself off while gathering his senses. He was mad at me for not helping him during the attack. He said, *"You just stood there and watched! You did not even try to help me!"* He angrily turned away from me and started walking to our next class.

I caught up to him as I apologized for letting him down. I told him that I was afraid of those guys, and I did not know how to help him. He said, *"Why didn't you ask your sister's boyfriend to take up for me, too?"* I told him that he had already left the area. He was still angry with me because I did not try to help him in any way. I felt ashamed of myself for being such a coward that was not there for my best friend.

A third time that I encountered the group of hazers was much like the second time. Me and one of my friends had just left the cafeteria. The old gymnasium on campus was used for a place to eat for those students that brought their lunches to school. It was a hang out area for most students that did not hang out by the smoke tree. We made our way along the sidewalk to the old gym, but the smoke tree was right there beside the side entrance to the gym. So, we decided to go around to the other entrance to avoid the hooligans near the tree.

When we rounded the corner of the gymnasium, we came face to face with the same bunch of guys that had initiated my other two friends. My sister's boyfriend was a senior, and he had already graduated which meant he was not at school. The hooligans said again, *"Well, well, well. Look who we have here! And your buddy is not here to save you this time!"*

The school year was coming to an end by now as they were desperate to initiate me. My friend that had accompanied me had already been initiated so they had no interest in him. They came after me and grabbed me the shirt to begin the ritual. All of a sudden, the side door entrance of the gymnasium came flying open with a loud bang. We were standing just outside of the gym right next to the door. The loud noise of the door startled all of us as the bullies froze in their tracks once again.

My other sister's boyfriend came strutting out of the gym to see the group grabbing me. He turned slowly to them and said, *"I know y'all ain't messing with my family! I am gonna tell his daddy about y'all and he will kick y'alls ass!"* He was probably the second strongest guy in the school so they released their grip from my shirt and walked away.

The group left me alone, but they made more threats as they departed. God saved me three different times from the agony of the red belly initiation. He worked through various people with impeccable timing and placement because they were in the right spot at the right time. A few days later my eldest sister's boyfriend asked me if the group of bullies were still threatening me at school.

I told him about the old gym incident as he listened in amazement. He said, *"I told them not to mess with my family!"* I asked him not to worry about them because I just wanted to get my initiation over with where I did not have to live in fear anymore. I would rather face the consequences instead of hiding everyday at school.

Later that week at school, the lead bully approached me in the hall. He said, *"We are good friends right? Me and you are good friends! Tell your sister's boyfriend that me and you are good buddies, and I won't mess with you anymore."* The bully informed me that my sister's boyfriend had pulled up to his car while he was parked at the store. He said that he got out of his car and started beating him up from outside the door.

The bully told me that my sister's boyfriend was punching him in the face while telling him, *"I told you not to mess with my family! I told you that he was my brother!"* Again the bully said, *"So, make sure that you let him know that we are good friends now!"* I made it through the whole school year without receiving my initiation.

I know that God protected me from further abuse because he knew what I had already gone through. The red belly initiation ritual ended that year. My senior class did not partake in any type of punishment towards the younger students. We just simply welcomed them to high school with respect and dignity.

CHAPTER 5
LOVE AND HATE

Basketball was one of my favorite sports. My family had a basketball goal in the backyard. I would go outside to shoot baskets for fun. I started drawing up these tournaments in my notebook that I would play out in the backyard. Some of the tournaments had as many as thirty two teams in them, and I would play out every game all the way to the championship game.

I would play like they were televised games in front of sold out arenas. My team of course was the number one team in the country, and I was the best player in the nation as well. I would act out the crowd, the announcer, the PA announcer and the entire starting five for all teams in the tournament.

It would take me hours sometimes just to come up with the teams and the players. However, I managed to memorize every player from every team as I would act out each tournament game with commentary and crowd reactions along with the referees calls along with the game clock and buzzer.

The PA announcer would begin each contest with the introductions of the starting line-ups. I could imagine a sold out stadium with thousands of screaming fans in attendance for these very prestigious events. I would dribble around the yard simulating game action when a shot was taken and made then that team scored. If the shot missed the mark, I would try to catch the ball before it reached the ground.

If I caught the ball before it reached the ground then I called it an offensive rebound, but if the ball touched the ground before I could reach it then it became a defensive rebound for the other team. That is how I kept up with which team had possession of the ball. I would usually play the first round games to ten or twenty points. Then advancing to the second round, those games would last until thirty points. Each round would continue to increase with points in the final score until the final championship game which usually went to fifty points.

I would play for hours in the backyard finishing those tournaments. I had so much fun using my imagination that time would just fly by during my activity. I believe the way that I practiced different scenarios helped me to become a better basketball player. I was already prepared for just about anything the game could throw at me.

I began attending church with my friend down the road. He was an adult that was married with a child on the way. His wife was pregnant and expecting their first child at any time. They invited me and my friends to go to church with them. They attended a small, rural church out in the country.

The church was small in size but big with love. The first time that I went there, I was greeted with so much love and joy. I was the last person standing as the preacher was waiting for me to sit down in order for him to begin the services. The members of the church kept calling me over to their pews to welcome me and to meet me while introducing me to their families.

I noticed the preacher waiting for me to take a seat when the preacher said, *"You are fine. You just go right ahead. We will wait."* I was embarrassed at this moment because the whole congregation was looking at me, and the man that had called me over said, *"I guess you better take your seat. They are waiting on us."* I quickly made my way to the pew where my friends were sitting as they laughed and giggled at me. The people at that church treated me with so much love that they made me feel pure joy from God.

They all invited me to return again as we departed from the services. The next Sunday on the way to church, I told my friends that I was going to go straight in and sit in my seat. I told them that I was not going to get embarrassed again by holding up the services, but that did not happen as they church members started calling me over to their pews again with more love and welcoming introductions. Again, I was the last one standing while the preacher was waiting on me.

I made my way back to the pew where my friends sat waiting and laughing at my embarrassment. On the way home from church, we discussed how I was the last one standing again. They said, *"God knows what you need! You must need all that love and attention. They did not call us over there, just you."* I realized at that moment that God was looking out for me once more.

I loved going to that church. Our youth group was outstanding as we won every youth rally that we attended. The group with the highest amount in attendance would get to fly their churches flag at the next rally. I learned many things at that church about family, togetherness, love, joy, and God. I memorized the books of the new testament from one of our Sunday school lessons, and they taught us how to acknowledge one another with loving respect.

They told us to ask others how they were doing. This was a genuine act of love when one inquired about another person's well-being. My best friend and I took this method and demonstrated it at school. We would walk down the hall acknowledging every person that we could possibly tend to.

Some people would respond pleasantly while others would give us a cussing. During this process, we noticed that nobody asked how we were doing. One night my best friend called me at home on the telephone. He asked me how I was doing.

I told him, *"You know that you are the first person that has asked me how I was doing in two weeks."* He responded to me saying, *"Nobody has still not asked me either."* So I quickly said, *"How are you doing?"* He said, *"That doesn't count. I called you and ask you."*

I told him all right then. I will call you tomorrow to ask you how you are doing. He said that he would be waiting to hear from me. I realized how I was thinking so selfishly that I had forgotten to ask my own best friend how he was doing. I had started to feel sorry for myself because nobody had inquired about my well-being.

I called my best friend the next day to ask him how he was doing. He laughed while thanking me for the kind gesture. I asked him if someone had beat me to the punch by asking him first about his well-being. He said, *"No. Nobody has still not asked me how I was doing."* I told him that nobody but him had asked me either.

As the school year drew closer to the end, my classmates wanted to plan an end of the year party. They wanted us all to camp out at the rock crusher. We were to ask our parents if could stay the night with one of our friends, but we were really going to stay out at the rock crusher.

On the last day of school of my eighth grade year nearly all of my classmates rode the bus to our friend's house that lived near the rock crusher. Several students had brought tents and camping supplies with them to school. We collected our money to give to one of our older brothers, and they acquired liquor and marijuana for our party.

I had never smoked marijuana before that night, but I had tried different liquors. We had beer, whiskey, vodka and a quarter of weed for the end of the year event. We all walked down the gravel road to the entrance of the rock crusher. We followed the path that led to a creek near the edge of the forest. It was in the back part of the rock crusher where we set-up camp.

All of the camping classmates were the boys of our class, but a few of the girls did come by to inquire about our activities. The girls did not drink much liquor nor did they smoke any marijuana because they all had to be home later that night. We had a campfire with several tents pitched for the night.

It was a memorable night for my friends and I as we sat around the campfire talking about the past school year. We learned a little bit more about each other as the night went on into the darkness. The heavy drinking of liquor caused several people to get sick while others became belligerent from the alcohol.

My best friend and I were forced to take care of the inept drinkers as we tended to the sick and disorderly. One of our classmates was so drunk that he got sad and stumbled to the edge of the rock crusher threatening to end his life. The cliff was about a one hundred foot drop-off to the bottom of the rock crusher.

We ran up to the edge to corral him and try to talk some sense into him. Thankfully, we got him to calm down as we escorted him back to camp. Evidently, he had gotten upset because one of the girls would not kiss him. So, he took off down the path by himself crying and sobbing over the girl, but he finally came to his senses once that he returned to camp.

I had a fun time at the party getting to know my classmates, but I also realized that taking care of belligerent drunk people was not much fun. My ninth grade year started off with me standing up to the bully of our class. Everybody would meet in the front of the high school on the first day of school. I wanted to ask my best friend about his class schedule. I saw him sitting in the middle of our classmates as I approached him to set down beside him.

My school was mostly white people, and in those days a lot of people were very racist. I noticed when I walked up on the group that the bully of our class was talking loudly while others were laughing. I did not pay much attention to him because I was wondering about my best friend's class schedule.

I could not get a word out of my mouth because the bully was constantly berating a new student. He was a black student that had moved into our town over the summer. He went on for several minutes with racial threats, racial jokes, and racially demeaning insults.

We were all just sitting there listening to him berate the new student because we were all afraid of him. I glanced over to see the new student crying over the verbal beat down. I felt so sorry for him at that moment that I felt something go through my body as I yelled out to the bully, *"Shut the fuck up!"*

The bully froze in his tracks with his mouth dropped wide open. He slowly turned to me and said, *"You're gonna take up for the nigger?"* I was afraid of the bully so I reluctantly answered, *"Yes. I guess that I am."* Then the bully said, *"Well, I guess that I will just have to whip your ass too!"*

One of my classmates stood up next to the new student and said, *"I am taking up for him too!"* That student was an overweight boy in our class who had never stood up to anybody before that day. The bully told him, *"What is your fat ass gonna do? Well, I'll just have to whip your fat ass too! As a matter of fact, I will whip all three of your asses!"*

The bell for school to start rang at that moment of the standoff. I still did not get to ask my best friend about his class schedule as we stood there staring at each other. The bully then told us, *"Y'all are saved by the bell, but I will get each one of you!"* He then turned away to walk into the front door of the high school.

Me and my friend that stood up for the new student along with the new student made our way to the front door as well. We were a few feet behind the bully when my friend ask me, *"Do you think that he will whip our asses?"* I replied to him, *"He ain't gonna do a damn thing to me!"* The bully heard me say that to my friend as he was going into the school. He turned to give me a bad look before entering the hallway.

The bully never did mess with my friend and I after that morning, but he did continue to berate and demean our new classmate. Until one day between classes the new student finally took up for himself. The bully tried to grab him one day out by the parking lot, but the new student managed to avoid his grasp by slipping out of his jacket.

The bully slung the jacket to the ground as he angrily went after our new classmate. He lunged and grabbed at the new student growing more angry with each failed attempt. The new student started swinging back at the bully out of fear. He landed a few punches to the bully's face all while the bully did nothing to him but stumble around trying to get his hands on him.

The bully became irate with anger as we urged on the new student to stand his ground. A teacher came out from the school as the bully continued to confront the new student. We dispersed from the scene with the knowledge of the teacher approaching the fight. So, the bully decided to calm down and walk away too before he got into any trouble for fighting. He never bullied that student again from that day forward. He just had to stand his ground and confront the bully to put an end to the abusive treatment.

That same year on the first day of basketball practice, we had to teach a lesson to the younger guys on the team. I was in the ninth grade with four of my classmates on the team too. We were all still warming up and waiting on our coach to tell us what to do in practice. We were on the junior high school team that was comprised of seventh, eighth, and ninth graders.

Coach was on the other end of the gymnasium tending to the seventh graders plans when the eighth graders approached my friends and I about an idea that had come up with for practice. They wanted to scrimmage our team against their team. They said, *"We were undefeated last year on the seventh grade team, and we won every tournament that we entered. And we think that we can beat y'all!"*

When our coach came over to us we informed him about their idea for practice. We said that they wanted to scrimmage us today. He looked around in confusion and said, *"So this was their idea?"* We said, *"Yes. They think that they can beat us!"* Coach agreed to the notion that we could scrimmage the eighth graders. He said, *"I was going to split y'all up into even teams, but I think this sounds like a good idea."*

We scrimmaged to twenty the first game with my team winning the contest twenty to nothing. They did not score one basket as we swarmed all over them defensively, and we were dominate on the offensive end as well. The second game of the scrimmage they managed to score one basket losing twenty to two. Finally, they lost the third segment of practice with yet another shutout!

The next day at practice our coach gathered the team around to ask if the eighth graders wanted to scrimmage our team again. They quickly answered no. They told coach that they had learned their lesson and that they were wanting to split up into even teams. He told them, *"Welcome to Junior High School. There is a big difference between seventh grade ball and junior high ball."* They answered coach, *"Yes. We agree. We found that out the hard way."*

I was on the track team later that spring. My coach entered me into seven events. I did not particularly enjoy running track, but our coach required us to join the track team in order for us to play on the basketball team. I was to compete in the 100 yard dash, the 200 yard dash, the 400 yard dash, the 400 yard dash relay, the 800 yard dash relay, the 1600 yard dash relay, and the long jump. I qualified for the finals in each event.

I did not win any of the events, but I did win a ribbon in every event that I entered. I was waiting for my turn in the long jump finals when I felt someone pecking on my shoulder. I turned around to see one of the managers from the team. He said, *"Everybody else is on the bus. Coach sent me to find you because we are about to leave."*

I told him that I was waiting for my turn in the long jump event. I was standing right next to the judges table *when* the manager approached me with the news, and a woman judge overheard our conversation. She said, *"I can put you down as a scratch if you need to leave."* I told her that I wanted to try to win the event.

I turned back around to tell the manager that I was going to take my turn on the long jump, but he was already gone back to the bus. I saw him leaving out the gate to the parking lot as I peered around the stadium. I noticed that everybody from my school was gone; even my parents were gone.

I looked back down at the female judge as she had noticed the manager leaving as well. She just gave me a sad look and slid the tenth place ribbon across the table to me. She said, *"I am so sorry. It looks like you do not have much of a choice."* I said to her, *"I can not believe this. They just left me."*

I grabbed the ribbon from the table, and I made my way out of the stadium. I saw the bus off in the distance with the lights on and the other members of the track team awaiting my arrival. I was so mad at my coach for leaving me out there by myself because I did not want to run track in the first place.

CHAPTER 6

LESSONS OF LIFE

My father wanted an activity for us both to share so we could spend more time together. He wanted to take me deer hunting for the first time. We went to the gun store and purchased some hunting rifles for our expedition. We started going out to the rock crusher to hone our shooting skills with target practice. He taught me how to adjust the sights on the barrel of a rifle to make sure that the rifle sights were true to center.

His rifle had a scope instead of sights, but his scope needed some adjustments as well. After a few weeks of preparation for our hunt, we left for deer camp in southern Arkansas. One of my father's friends had some land in Monticello, Arkansas where he and his two sons had hunted for several years. He invited my father and I to join them for the annual retreat.

The camp was fairly primitive with just the basic needs for survival. They did have an old school bus that had been transformed into some type of a camper. There was a wood burning stove in the bus which supplied the heat for the cold nights, and there were several cots for the hunters to sleep that filled the rest of the bus.

We did an afternoon scout of the forest while they pointed out the tree stands that my father and I were to use for the hunt. The older men of the camp stayed up late that night drinking beer and telling tales well into the evening, and the younger boys were restricted to the old school bus. I could not sleep that night as I watched the adult men perched around the campfire having the time of their life.

I was awoken by my father early that morning before the sunrise. It was important to be in your tree stand before the sun would rise in the sky. I was led to my stand first as I watched the others disappear into the dark forest. It was scary in those dark woods all by yourself. I began to hear all kinds of strange sounds and noises coming from the ground below me, but I could not see what was making the sounds.

Much to my delight, the sun finally rose in the sky. I was afraid and freezing when the light from the sun provided me with warmth and security. I sat there in that stand for a few hours without seeing one deer. I did see a few squirrels and some birds though. It felt like forever out there in the forest when I needed to use the bathroom. So, I made the decision to leave the tree stand and head back to the camp. They did not have a bathroom at the camp, but I was looking to find some toilet paper.

The camp was empty upon my return as everybody else was still in the forest. I could not find any toilet paper to use, but I had to use the bathroom then and there. So, I went over to use the bathroom by an old abandoned shack that was near the camp. After I had finished using the bathroom, I stood up and took one step towards the camp.

I heard a loud popping noise when I took that first step, but I did not know where the noise had come from. When I took off walking away from the old shack, I noticed a plank of wood stuck to the bottom of my boot. At first, I thought that the wood was stuck in the mud or something because I had not felt any pain. I reached down to my boot and grabbed the plank of wood with my hand to remove it, but the plank of wood did not move.

At that moment, I felt a nail up in my foot when I had grabbed the plank. Suddenly, I realized what that loud popping noise was that I had heard earlier. I looked around for help with the nail in my foot, but there was nobody around to come to my aid. I knew that I was going to have to pull that nail out of my foot by myself.

I reached down and grabbed the plank twisting it slowly. I had intended to remove the nail with a slow, deliberate motion, but I felt the pain from the nail when I twisted the plank. I knew then that I would have to pull it out quickly as I looked around the camp in panic.

There was still nobody around when I grabbed the plank and yanked the nail out of my foot with one quick motion. I yelled out in pain as I freed the nail out of my foot. I looked at the wood plank to see an old rusty nail that was two or three inches long. In disgust, I threw the wood plank out into the woods. I was confused and hurt when I made the decision to go find my father in the forest.

I knew the general vicinity of his tree stand from the scout that we had done the previous day. About halfway down the trail, I ran into my father coming down the trail. He was in a rushed frenzy when I encountered him on the trail. He said, *"I have shot a deer and I need help with it!"* I told him that I had stepped on a nail, but the deer took precedence over the situation.

He told me that we would look at my foot later after we tended to the shot deer. I was not in a great deal of pain, but I was afraid because of the rust on the nail. He told me that I should be fine from the injury, but I might need to get a tetanus shot when we get back home. I told him that I was all right, and that I would help him with the deer.

As we made our way down the trail, he told me that the deer was still alive when he left his tree stand. He had actually shot two deer, but he could not find one of them. As we approached his tree stand, I saw the wounded deer which had been shot through the spinal cord with one bullet while the second bullet impacted the deer's face.

The deer was dragging itself around with its front legs while its back legs where paralyzed from the gunshot that had severed its spinal cord. The deer's lower jaw was hanging from its mouth as a result of the second shot. It was a gruesome site that I was not prepared for as we approached the wounded animal. We searched for a short while for the other deer that had left a blood trail, but we lost the trail and could find the second deer.

We returned to the other deer to find it still alive. My father said, *"We need to put it out of its misery! We need to shoot it where it want be in pain anymore!"* I told my father that I would shoot the deer to end its pain. I felt so sorry for the creature as it cried out in pain trying to escape our presence.

My father handed me his pistol and told me to end the anguishing saga. I took the pistol and aimed point blank at the deer's head when all of a sudden the deer lifted its front leg and covered its face. I was shaking from the fear and panic as I pulled the trigger. The pistol fired off loudly as the deer did not move an inch. My father said to me, *"Did you miss? I think you missed!"*

He took the pistol from my hand and put it against the deer's head. He pulled the trigger and the deer fell over to the side from the impact of the bullet. The deer quickly raised its head back up from the ground letting out a loud bellowing noise almost like a sound from a cow. I thought blood and guts would go flying everywhere but that was not the case.

Finally, the deer fell back over to the side and laid there breathing slower and slower. The poor animal had been shot three times and was still fighting for its life. My father said, *"We need to cut its throat now so it doesn't suffer any longer."* He pulled out his knife and cut the deer's throat while it was still alive.

The deer still laid there breathing and dying after its throat was cut. The cut in the throat severed the creatures wind pipe as I could see steam coming from the opening in its throat every time that the animal would breathe. We made our way back to camp to retrieve the truck so we could get the deer out of the woods.

When we returned to the deer, the creature had finally died as we loaded the animal into the truck. Once that we returned to camp, we had to field dress the deer. Basically, we had to cut the animal's guts out of it. Then, we strung up the deer to skin it as I had forgotten all about my foot injury due to the commotion with the deer. Many hours had gone by when I removed my boot to look at my wound. I had a blood stain on my sock about the size of a half dollar.

We stayed another night at camp before departing for home that next morning. My father was worried about my foot injury so we chose to leave camp a day early. He let me drive all the home that day which was about a three to four hour drive back to the house. That weekend with my father served as a bonding of our friendship that would last for many years.

That year is when I started sneaking out at night. I would wait for the rest of my family to go to bed, and I would ease out the back door very quietly. My father had bought me a motorcycle earlier that year, and I would push the motorcycle around to the front yard. Then, I would push it down the road to start the engine.

I did not want my parents to hear the noisy motor as I drove away in the night. I would just ride around to feel the wind against my face. The freedom from the open highway seemed almost therapeutic. It did feel odd and scary since everybody else was asleep.

I would ride by all of my friend's houses only to see that all of their lights were turned off. The whole town was asleep as I drove around on my motorcycle. I often wondered why I was still awake and running around town like some rebel. I pondered on why I was so different than everybody else.

One night, I drove my motorcycle down an old country road. A creek ran under the road in that area which was named ten mile creek. It was ten miles from town. My motorcycle just shut down all of a sudden and the engine stopped running. It was very dark out there in the middle of nowhere when my headlight had also gone out when the engine stalled. I had ran out of gas.

Fear and panic went through my body as my heart was racing in my chest. There were no houses for several miles. The houses that I did happen to see would have been asleep anyway, and I could not call home because I was supposed to be in bed asleep too. Therefore,

I did not have anyone to call even if I found a house that would let me use their telephone.

Suddenly, I remembered my father telling me about the reserve fuel line under the gas tank. He told me that the reserve tank should last about twenty miles. I reached down by the engine to twist the lever to the reserve position as I prayed that was the solution. I gave a couple of kick starts but the engine still did not start.

Finally, the third try was the charm as the engine fired right up with the headlight illuminating the darkness once again. I took off driving back home as fast as I could with the hopes of reaching familiar territory before running out of gas again. Fortunately, the reserve tank had enough fuel to get me all the way home that night. I never felt so happy to see my house. The security and safety of one's home and family is priceless.

That summer is when my best friend started working as a brick laborer. He was hired by a brick mason crew that worked in Little Rock, Arkansas. The crew would lay brick on new homes with the bricklayers constructing the brick wall while my best friend's duties were to supply the bricklayers with their materials.

He would take them their bricks and mortar while making sure that they did not run out of supplies. He would carry as many bricks as possible in order to minimize his trips during the day. He would also mix the mortar in a mixing machine which required him to pour fifty pound bags of sand into the mechanism along with water. The workers called the mixture; "mud."

It seemed to be a very physical job that required heavy lifting while working outside in the heat of the summer. He would wake up every morning and walk to the interstate near our neighborhood where the crew would pick him up for work. He would ride to work with the older men each day, and they would drop him off on the other side of the interstate on their way back home.

My best friend loved brick laboring with the men as I watched him mature over the summer. He got stronger from the tough work as the interaction with the adult men helped him to mature well beyond his years. He would always give a certain amount of his paycheck to his mother every time that he got paid. He said. *"I always give my mother some money to help with the bills, and the rest is for me to spend."* She was a single mother that worked a full-time job at a local factory.

He told me that it was his responsibility to earn money for their family. He enjoyed working and helping his mother, and he still found the time to practice basketball. I played my last year of pony league baseball that summer, and I would see him in their yard shooting basketball everyday as I drove by his house.

I never heard him complain one time about working. He had such a good attitude and outlook on life. He would share his hard earned money with friends as on several occasions he would have no money remaining by Monday after being paid on Friday. He said, *"I don't care about that money. I get paid again on Friday, and I've got lunch for all week."*

His muscles grew larger while the outdoor job tanned his skin as he transformed right before my eyes. His newfound strength and maturity helped him on the basketball court as well. I could see a vast improvement in my friend when we practiced at the gymnasium. Our coach would open the gym through the summer every Tuesday, Thursday, and Sunday night, and we never missed one practice. We were heading into the tenth grade that coming up school year which would be our first year on the senior high school basketball team.

A few weeks before school was scheduled to start, my best friend wanted to throw a party. His mother was going out of town for the weekend, and she had given him approval for the party since he had been so responsible over the summer. He bought everything for the party; food, beer, liquor, and weed.

He invited every person that he could think of as he wanted to have a memorable event. He even invited my ex-girlfriend to the party. He asked me, *"Would it make you mad if I invited your ex-girl-friend to the party?"* I told him that it did not bother me because we were not going together anymore. I said to him, *"Why did you invite her? I don't like her anymore."*

He quickly responded, *"Because I like her!"* He told me that he saw her at the store and invited her to the party, but they did not want to offend me. So, he wanted to know if I would give them my blessing. I told him that I was fine with them dating, and I appreciated him communicating the facts with me.

The party was a huge success with many people arriving from different age groups. My best friend and my ex-girlfriend made a beautiful couple. I saw them sitting at the kitchen table laughing and smiling at each other. He had his arm around her as he looked happier than I had ever seen him before. I walked up to the table and I told them. *"You guys look good together. Y'all make a good couple."*

They both said, *"Well, thank you. That means so much to us because we really like each other, but we did not want to hurt you."* I told them that I was happy for them both. I spent the night with my best friend that night as the party went on for hours. My best friend woke me up the next morning with the telephone in his hand. His family had a phone in the kitchen with a very long cord that would stretch all the way down the hall.

He said, *"It's your father! He wants to talk to you!"* I told him to tell my father that I was still asleep. He just gave me a sarcastic look while handing the phone to me. I got on the telephone to speak to my father and he said to me, *"What in the hell have you been doing all night? I got up to go to the store to get a newspaper, and when I drove by your friend's house there were beer cans in the yard and on the roof of the house. Get your ass home now because you are in trouble!"*

I handed the telephone back to my friend as he disconnected the conversation with my father. He said, *"Are you in trouble? He sounded mad."* I told him that I had to go home because he had driven by his house and saw a bunch of beer cans outside. My parents grounded me for two weeks for my punishment.

My best friend cleaned the entire house and yard before his mother returned home from her weekend getaway. He did not get into any trouble from his mother because she said that he had taken care of the house like a responsible young man.

My best friend and I started smoking marijuana more and more that summer. By the time that school had rolled around, we were smoking pot everyday. We would get high and go to basketball practice during the summer. I did not like going around authority figures after smoking marijuana because I was afraid that we would get in trouble.

The marijuana always made us feel paranoid and nervous when we went to the gym for basketball practice. My best friend acted like the weed did not bother him one bit. I was watching him at practice as he ran up and down the court laughing and smiling without a care in the world, but I was very scared and nervous that our coach could tell that we were high.

It seemed like we played basketball better when we were high for some reason. My body felt odd when I would shoot the ball. I would yell out "off" every time that I took a shot, but the ball would rip right through the net instead. I heard my friend calling off on his shots too, but his shots were ripping the net as well.

We were making every shot that we took, and I looked at my friend running down the court loving life with a big smile on his face. He was wearing a red headband, and I noticed that his eyes were just as red as his headband. He noticed me watching him from across the court as he said to me, *"It makes you better!"*

From that moment on, I started to relax more when playing high because nobody could tell if we were high or not. If anyone thought that we were high they must have been confused because we played basketball so good. Some of our teammates could tell that we were high, but our coach never said a word to us about smoking marijuana.

That school year we would smoke pot before our first period class. We would ride around in one of our cars smoking weed right before school started then we would dart into class at the last possible moment. We carried around Visine for the red eyes, cologne for the smell, and chewing gum for our breath.

The first time that we smoked marijuana before school was

before math class. Our basketball coach was the teacher of that class as I was afraid of getting caught. We lost track of time that morning as we rode around town near the campus. My best friend and I were nearly late for class because we both had to stop by our lockers to retrieve our math book.

We quickly made our way down the hall to see our coach standing in the doorway holding the door. We had to pass in front of him very closely as we entered the classroom but he did not notice any hint of the marijuana. The pot did make the class more interesting while also improving our attention to detail. It made life feel more fun and appealing.

That same year on the basketball team we had a total of ten people that signed up for the team. We had two seniors, five juniors, and three sophomores that comprised the roster. Everything seemed to be running fairly smooth during the first few weeks of practice. We had good practices and everyone got along well with each other.

We had a good starting line-up that was comprised of two seniors, two juniors, and one sophomore. My best friend's sudden maturity growth had catapulted him into the starting line-up. He was one of our taller players standing around six feet and three inches in height. He had always been a tall, lanky specimen but then he transformed with his newfound muscle gain from his summer job. He was now a tall, strong young man that had vastly improved his basketball skills as well.

Our second team was a good team too. We would beat the starting five often during practice. The starters even commented on how good the team would be in the coming year because of our quality depth. The second team was comprised of three juniors, and two sophomores as we entered the season with high hopes.

I thought that everybody was happy with their roles. We won our first two games of the season with every member of the team playing significant minutes in each game. Until one day at practice, we noticed that our coach along with three of the juniors on the team were late coming out to the court.

They finally came out of the locker room area when our coach called all of us over to the bleachers for a discussion. That is when he informed us about the three junior's bitterness concerning their roles on the team. Coach retrieved the score book to show us that we all had played the same amount of minutes both games. They were still not satisfied with sharing the minutes on the team as they continued to argue their stance.

Our coach asked them if they expected to be in the starting line-up. They said that all the starters deserved to start, but they were not happy coming off of the bench. Coach informed them that he started the players which gave us the best chance at winning the game. The three disgruntled juniors had not attended any of the summer practices while the seven other teammates never missed one practice all summer.

We had worked hard all summer long practicing with each other while improving our continuity. Coach told them that we deserved to play because we had earned that right from committing to the team during the summer. One of the juniors told coach, "We *can't make it to the practices because we have to work. Some people do have jobs you know.*"

At that time our coach turned to my best friend and asked him, "*You've been working all summer haven't you?*" My best friend hung his head because he did not want to offend the three juniors. Our coach continued with my best friend as he said, "As *a matter of fact, you worked in Little Rock didn't you? And you did not miss a single practice.*"

The next day at practice the three juniors were not present as our coach was late arriving once again. He came out of his office to inform us that they had quit the team, and that he might lose his job too. One of the junior's father was the president of the school board, and coach had to fight to keep his job before the school board review committee. The departure of the three juniors left the team with just seven players remaining on the team.

We did not have enough people left on the team to run a scrim-mage practice. So, my best friend and I along with the third sophomore approached the remaining upperclassmen left on the team with the notion of giving up our spots on the team. We told them that we were going to tell coach about our idea. We knew the importance of having the three juniors on the team was pertinent to our success.

The upperclassmen advised us not to offer that notion to the coach because we had earned our spots from dedication and commitment to the team. Our coach was still in his office so we decided to approach him with our solution. We knocked on the office door as he welcomed us into the office.

He appeared to be under a great deal of stress as he sat at his desk. He asked us, *"What are y'all doing in here? What do y'all want?"* We answered to him, *"We want to give our spots to the juniors that quit because we need them on the team."* He said, *"That is very noble of you guys to offer that for the team, but I am the coach and it is my decision on who plays and when they play. My job as a coach is to win ball games or I could get fired. So, I play the people that will give me the best chance of winning. Those three juniors are lucky to have teammates like you guys."*

Our coach told us to go back out to the court with our other teammates to wait on him, and he thanked us for offering such a selfless notion. We returned to the court where the upperclassmen eagerly waited for our return as they asked us about our meeting with the coach. We told them that he said no to our idea as they started giving each other high fives saying, *"We knew it, we knew it!"*

Now the team was comprised *of two seniors, two juniors, and three sophomores. Our coach entered the gym floor that day to tell us about his school board meeting later that night. He said, "I don't know what is going to happen. I may not be back tomorrow. They are trying to get me fired over this."*

We gathered for the next practice not knowing what had transpired from the school board meeting when our coach came walking out from the office. He said, *"They quit the team, and they will not be coming back to the team. I am the coach here and It is my responsibility to decide on who gives us the best chance of winning. That is what I have always done and that is what I will continue to keep doing. I don't care what your father or mother does for a living. I only care about putting the best team that I can out on the floor."*

Our coach found an eighth member for the team. We had a new student that was in the ninth grade, but he was supposed to be in tenth grade. He was in the special education class when coach found out about him. He was a big boy with size and girth which the team needed. We would use the managers or junior high players to give us ten people in order to help us practice and scrimmage.

The start of the White County tournament our coach told us that we were the lowest seeded team in the tournament which meant that we had to play the highest seeded team right off the bat. Our coach informed us that all of the other coaches were feeling sorry for us because we only had eight players on the team.

I did not start that year, but I played a vital role for the team. I was always on the court at the end of the games as I was the first man off the bench. My best friend played amazingly as he led our team to the first round upset of the top seed in the tournament. Our team went on to win the White County tournament that year.

It was the first time in thirty years that our school had taken the title. My best friend was voted to the All-Tournament team, and he received the most valuable player of the tournament as well. He was only a sophomore that year while accomplishing these feats. We cut down the nets and hoisted the trophy before our adoring fans while spraying grape juice all over each other as we celebrated our triumphant tournament success.

We played the number one team in the state from our classification later that same year. Our coach showed us a newspaper article that showed their record of 33-0 and their ranking which was number one. We played them on their home court as the game went down to the wire. My best friend and I both tallied a triple double stat line that night.

My best friend accumulated 35 points, 22 rebounds, and 10 assist while I tallied 14 points, 15 assist, and 10 rebounds in the game. With 15 seconds left in the game, we trailed the top ranked team by one point. I stole the ball from their star point guard while making my way down the court for a lay-up.

The basket would have put us ahead in the game, but I heard the referee's whistle blow right when I was laying the ball in the basket. The referee had called me for a travel even though I had only taken one step after picking up my dribble. My coach ran out onto the court to dispute the bad call when the referee called him for a technical foul. The resulting technical gave the other team two free throw attempts and possession of the ball.

We were still down by one with seven seconds to go in the game when they missed both of the free throw attempts. Then, they could not inbounds the ball which caused the referees to call a five second violation on their team which gave our team possession of the ball again. We still had a chance to win the game. Our coach called a timeout and designed a play for us to inbound the ball.

The play was designed for me to get the ball. Coach said, *"When you come off of the two screens you should be open. Then pivot around and take the shot. You should be wide-open."* As we broke the huddle, I heard my coach say to me, *"Watch for the high post. Its been open all night."* I nodded to coach to let him know that I understood his design.

The high post area was where my best friend played and he was playing very well that night. I ran through the two screens of my teammates to receive the inbound ball, and I pivoted around to face the basket. And just like coach had said, I was wide-open. As I squared up to shoot the basketball, I noticed my best friend in the high post area near the free throw line waving his hand around. He was wide-open too. So, I threw him the ball since he had scored so many points in that game.

He rose in the air to shoot the basketball, but then at the last second he passed the ball right under the goal. One of our seniors was wide-open for a lay up, but he panicked due to the lack of time on the clock. He struggled to gain control of the ball as he attempted to shoot the lay up.

He managed to get the shot away before the buzzer sounded, but he missed the whole goal shooting an air ball. I watched as our senior fell to the ground in dismay as the game drew to an end. I approached my best friend at the free throw line and said, *"Why didn't you take the shot? You have been hot all night!"* He then answered me back, *"Why didn't you take the shot? Coach told you to take the shot!"*

I quickly replied to him saying, *"Coach told me to watch the high post, and I saw that you were open!"* He replied, *"I went to shoot it, but I saw our senior open!"* He pointed to that senior at that moment of the conversation. We noticed him still on the floor just sitting there listening to every word we said to each other. We realized that we were not being good teammates as we selfishly blamed one another for our defeat. Our senior teammate noticed us looking at him and said, *"No, no, no! Y'all go right ahead with y'alls little conversation!"*

We quickly made our way over to the fallen senior as I held out my hand to him, but he slapped my hand away in disgust saying, *"Get the hell away from me! I can stand up on my own!"* My best friend and I departed the court with our fellow teammates as we knew that we should have won the game. My best friend's triple double was one of the best performances I have ever witnessed.

Our basketball team finished the season with a 22-8 record despite only having eight players on the roster. My best friend had an outstanding season as he was named to the dream team. A team chosen from the local coaches from the county which was featured in the local newspaper each year. The dream team was typically comprised of upperclassmen that were the top basketball players from our county and surrounding areas. It was a rare feat for an underclassmen to achieve such an honor.

The highest praise awarded to my best friend was when he was chosen as the dream team player of the year in just his sophomore campaign. His growth and maturation began earlier that summer when he started working as a brick laborer as he perfected the art of basketball on his own time. His stellar play led our team to accomplish feats that many teams before us had not fulfilled.

My best friend worked as a brick laborer again that next summer as the basketball team continued to improve. We practiced every time our coach would open the gym. Our team would scrimmage a men's team from the local adult league all summer long. We beat them handily every night as the men were astonished with our play. They told us, *"Y'all are going to be very good this year! We just won the men's league and y'all are destroying us!"*

We did not even realize how good we had become until that moment. We were just living life and having fun. The men's team members said that they were excited about our upcoming season as they planned to watch every game that we played. We knew that we were a good team, but we did not talk much about our goals.

My best friend and I were set to be juniors upon the beginning of the school year along with a third classmate. We were three juniors that accompanied two seniors in the prospective starting line-up for the upcoming season. That team was the best unit I had ever graced the court with because we had an unspoken connection between us from the many hours of practice time that we had shared together. We anticipated a historic season as we eagerly awaited the start of school.

CHAPTER 7

MISTAKES AND TRAGEDY

The school year came around as we continued to smoke marijuana and attend class. We smoked more and more each day as we fell deeper into our addiction. One night in particular, my best friend and I along with a classmate of ours smoked a whole ounce of marijuana. We parked down at the rock crusher and rolled 47 joints from the ounce of weed.

We went to our friend's uncle's house to stay the night where we smoked every joint before sunrise. The night flew by in a haze as we laughed and smoked with one another. I developed a major headache from the constant smoking as the sun rose in the early morning sky. We did not eat anything all night long, and we did not sleep at all the entire night.

I do not know why we abused ourselves the way we did that night. Perhaps it was out of sheer boredom, or maybe we were just thrill seekers looking for a good time. The constant running around everyday and smoking marijuana began to take a toll on us as we struggled with our daily responsibilities. My best friend and I were falling asleep in our classes, and we were failing in several classes too. We had several discussions about quitting the drug use because we knew that our futures were in jeopardy.

Until one day, I took my best friend home after school. It was a normal day much like any other day. We had basketball practice that evening, and we planned on riding to practice together as he stepped out of my car. He said, *"I will see you later. Stop by and pick me up for practice. And thanks for the ride."* I saw him running up his driveway as I drove down the road to my house.

I washed my car out in the driveway when I got home from school. My father was still at work, and my mother was not at home either. I had started cleaning the inside of my car when I noticed a strange vehicle pulling into the driveway. It was my neighbor's girlfriend who had come to tell me something. She asked me if my friend had a motorcycle, and I told her that none of my friends had a motorcycle.

She informed me that something had happened on the highway, and I needed to go with her. So, we left in her car driving down the road. As we approached the scene, I noticed several police cars and an ambulance parked on the side of the road. A crowd of people were already gathered at the scene. I approached the scene with much confusion when I witnessed one of my friends laying there on the ground writhing in pain.

I noticed a big street motorcycle wrecked near my friend as he cried out in agony, *"Daddy, Daddy! Where is my daddy!"* The paramedics were tending to him when one of the bystanders approached me. They told me that my best friend was riding the motorcycle too, and the first ambulance had already left with him to the hospital.

The onlooker told me that my best friend was in bad shape as the paramedics rushed him away in the ambulance. Evidently, they had ran wide in the curve and lost control of the motorcycle. That section of the highway had very high embankments on each side of the road because of the interstate overpass that was near the curve. They had careened down a steep fifty foot drop-off after running off of the highway.

I asked my neighbor's girlfriend to take me back home. I needed to check on my friend at the hospital. I drove my car one hundred miles per hour on the way to the hospital. I was so worried about his condition. I was shocked to see that half of the town was already there upon my arrival. My mother was there among the crowd. I saw her down the hall sitting with my best friend's mother and his little brother as they waited in fear of the unknown.

My mother had seen me down the hallway when she approached me with a hug. I could tell that she was scared from the way that she squeezed me. She said to me, *"He is in bad shape. I was one of the first people to arrive at the accident site. I found him laying on the ground, and he was barely breathing with blood coming out of his ear."*

At that moment, I felt this overwhelming fear come over my entire body. I never thought about his death. I was thinking that maybe he would only miss a few games of basketball. She said that the doctors had come out and told his mother that he was on a life support machine, and the prognosis for his recovery was dim.

His little brother talked to me about how the accident transpired. He told me that they were going to town for some sunflower seeds. My classmate wanted to take my best friend riding on his uncle's motorcycle so they took off to the store. His little brother knew something had happened when they did not return. He was standing out in the yard listening to the motorcycles engine as he watched them drive out of sight. He said that the noisy engine could not be heard after they had gone over the bridge.

He saw some flashing lights across the interstate and ran down the highway to investigate. Upon his arrival, he was shocked to see that they had wrecked in the curve. His brother had been thrown a hundred feet from the motorcycle. The doctors thought that he had landed on his head which pushed his spinal cord into his brain. I never felt so alone and afraid at that moment as the news about my best friend kept getting worse.

The crowd of people that lined the hallways of the hospital waited for hours that night with the hopes of good news from the doctors. I saw the doctors call in his family, but when they returned from the visit they were all very upset. It did not take long for the news to travel down the hall to me that my best friend had died.

He was only sixteen years old when he passed away from the tragic accident. I nearly collapsed from the news as I watched everybody else crying out in anguish. His mother was devastated as she wept uncontrollably. I had lost the one true person in my life that cared about me. My teammate, my classmate, my best friend was gone forever. In the blink of an eye, my whole world changed from a paradise into a nightmare. We did everything together as we relished each other's company.

I could not fathom a life without him by my side. He was my strength and courage as he always showed me respect and support. He made life fun and happy everyday for the blessed people that were able to spend time with him. I have never recovered from losing my friend that day as I still long for his return.

Before I could leave the hospital, a group of doctors came up to me and asked if I would check on our other friend that was involved in the wreck. Most of our classmates were still at the hospital when we decided to visit him as a group. The doctors informed us that our other friend could die too. He was in bad shape from the shock along with some broken bones and bruises.

The doctors asked us to not let him know about our other friend's death fearing that the tragic news could kill him, but it was very important that we show him some love and support in order for him to recover from the shock. About twenty of my classmates went upstairs to our friends' hospital room per doctor's orders, and the first words out of his mouth were concerning our fallen friend.

He said, *"How is our friend? Is he o.k.?"* I paused for a moment as I looked around the room at my classmates. Everyone of them were silent as well as they were all looking straight at me for the answer. I had just finished crying downstairs but somehow I held myself together long enough to answer my friend.

I told him that our other friend was still back in the emergency room as we were still awaiting news concerning his condition. I could tell that he knew I was lying when he stared deep into my eyes. I tried to hide the pain from him while I protected his fragile condition. He responded, *"Well, I hope that he is all right because I am worried about him."*

I continued to console my battered friend for several more minutes as my other classmates set there in silence. Once we left his room, the rest of my classmates thanked me for handling the situation so well. They said, *"We don't know how you did it. We did not know what to say. Thank you and we are sorry."*

We all left the hospital to return to our homes. I could not sleep that night as I laid in bed crying over my loss. I eventually cried myself to sleep. I awoke the next morning which was a school day only to find out that school had been canceled. I felt so alone and empty not knowing what to do for the day. I would usually call my best friend, but he was not there anymore. I drove by my best friend's house to see many cars parked at his house. My mother was there visiting as well. So, I stopped in for a visit to see what was going on. The adults were gathered around the dining room table planning my best friend's funeral. The same dining room table where he was sitting only a few months earlier at his party. I went down the hall and went into his room. I looked around for a few seconds wanting to catch some type of feeling from him, but I felt uncomfortable being in his room without him. I did not acquire any sense or feelings of spirituality from my beloved friend.

I departed from my best friend's house, and I drove to the hospital to visit with our other friend. I still could not let him know that our friend had died, but the doctors stressed the importance of our visits. So, I had to lie to him again that day. It was very difficult not telling him the truth because I could tell that he knew I was lying to him, but he never told me that he could tell I was lying for some reason

He was still in bad shape from the accident, and I guess it would have been unbearable for him to admit to the truth. He was still in the hospital the day of the funeral. School was canceled for the rest of the week as we were scheduled to return that next Monday. I had visited him for three straight days all while hiding the truth from my friend. I kept telling him that my best friend was hurt, and that he was in a hospital room recovering. The day of the funeral, I planned to visit the hospital after the services.

His funeral was a massive event that was held in the high school gymnasium. It seemed like the whole town was there as one side of the gymnasium was packed with people. I was a pallbearer along with the other members of the basketball team. We sat in chairs that were placed on the gymnasium floor right next to the members of his family.

It was a beautiful service that honored his life which was full of kind acts and commendable achievements. I did not know that he had impacted so many people in such a short time. He was buried across the street from the high school at the local cemetery with a graveside service. Near the end of the service, the pallbearers passed by his coffin and left a flower on top of it. I was the last one to pass by as I stopped for a minute to talk to my best friend one last time.

I told my best friend, *"Goodbye, good buddy. I am gonna miss you. You are the best friend that I have ever had."* At that time, I noticed his father standing next to the casket waiting for me to finish. His father was in prison at the time of the accident as he was standing there in a white prison jump suit with armed guards on each side. I quickly moved away so his father could have some time with his son.

He was only allowed a short time to view the coffin before the armed guards whisked him away back to prison in a police car. I was one of the last people to leave the cemetery that day as I found myself wondering what to do. I decided to check on our classmate in the hospital. I went straight to the hospital from the funeral, and I forgot to change my clothes. Somehow, my hospitalized friend knew of the funeral.

As soon as I walked into the room, he said, *"The funeral was today wasn't it? I can tell by how you are dressed. How was it?"* He continued to inform me about other things as well. He said to me, *"I knew that you were lying to me all along. I could see it in your eyes, but I know that you were only trying to protect me from the heartache. Thank you for being such a good friend. I know this must have been very difficult for you because he was your best friend."*

My classmate was released from the hospital a few days later as school commenced once again. He had healed fairly well from his injuries except for a broken arm, but he did not return to school. Life seemed like a nightmare for me after my friend's death, but I had to stay strong for my family and friends. A week of school had passed and our friend had still not returned.

My classmates and I thought that he was still recovering from his injuries. Our principal called me and two other classmates to the office one day to discuss some important news. He told us that our classmate was severely depressed as his father had grown very concerned about his son's mental health. His father told the principal that his son would not eat or come out of his room. The principal asked us three to go out and visit our classmate to pick up his spirit.

This particular classmate was the class bully that we all feared. Therefore, we did not like him much. But we agreed to visit with him anyway. Our principal instructed us to tell him that everybody was missing him at school, but we did not miss the bully tactics which he inflicted on us all everyday. My school was full of kind, loving people that truly cared for his well being and vitality.

After school that day, my two classmates rode with me to visit our friend. His father answered the door and welcomed us into his home. He thanked us for coming out to check on his son. Then, he told us to go down the hall to the last door on the left. The door was closed as we approached the end of the hall. I knocked on the door, but no one answered.

His father yelled down the hallway from the kitchen, *"Just go on in!"* He seemed very agitated and worried about his son's demeanor. I reluctantly twisted the doorknob and opened the door. We walked in his bedroom to see him sitting in a rocking chair. He was turned away from us just staring at the corner of the wall with a cover over his body. He sat there rocking back and forth in silence as we acknowledged him.

We told him that everybody at school was missing him as we were all waiting for his return. Suddenly, he spoke to us without ever making eye contact as he stared at the wall. He said, *"What are y'all even doing out here! I know that y'all don't even like me! I pick on all three of y'all everyday and I know that y'all hate me!* We stood there in silence not knowing how to respond to him as he continued to look away from us.

Then, he said to us, *"But it means a lot to me that y'all came out here, and I really appreciate the effort. Shut the door on y'alls way out!"* We told him goodbye and that we wanted to see him at school soon as we departed the bedroom. His father was pacing around the kitchen as we travelled down the hallway. He eagerly approached us with curiosity about our visit with his son.

He said, *"How did it go? What did he say? Did he talk to y'all?"* We told him that it went well as he had spoken to us about our friendship. His father thanked us again for coming out and trying to help his son. He said that he had tried everything that he could think of but nothing was working. So, he called the school for help out of desperation.

I was informed about the bullies past that evening from another classmate of mine. I had great empathy for him as I learned more about the many traumatic events that he had experienced as a child. His mother had committed suicide in the same bedroom that he was sitting in when we had visited with him. A short time before her death, his little brother had died too. They were driving down the road in a pickup truck with my classmate along with his little brother who were riding in the bed of the truck. As the truck went around a curve something happened and his little brother fell out of the back of the truck.

He landed on the highway and busted his head on the pavement. My classmate had to hold his little brother's head wound closed on the way to the hospital. His little brother died from the injuries to his head, and his mother could not take the pain and anguish of losing her child. So, she took her own life a short time after the accident.

Furthermore, he wrecked with my best friend that resulted in a third death for him to deal with. I understood why his father was so concerned about his son. In a span of a few years, the tragedy and sorrow that their family had endured was more than anyone should have to face in a lifetime. Suddenly, I understood that all of his bully tactics were actually an outlet of pain for him.

Much to my surprise, our injured classmate returned to school a few days after our visit. He thanked us for visiting him and lifting his spirit enough to try again. He became a good friend of mine after learning about his past. I saw him in a different light from that day forward. I was mad at him as I blamed him for my best friend's death, but I know that he did not mean hurt my friend because of the excessive tragedies that he had already experienced. The last thing that he wanted was another death to deal with as he already struggled with the trauma from his past.

CHAPTER 8

LIVING WITH LOSS

I continued to smoke marijuana after my best friend's death. I used the drug for a crutch to hide my true feelings. I smoked more and more everyday all while slipping away from reality. The only two things that I cared about was smoking pot and basketball. Even though neither of which was fun anymore with my side-kick gone.

I smoked marijuana before school, during school, after school, before basketball practice, and even before the basketball games. I stayed high everyday with no one doing anything about my drug use. Somehow, I managed to keep my grades above passing while playing basketball at an all star level. The year that my best friend died our basketball team was set for a historic season. Our summer practices had propelled our team into a dynamic unit, but the death of our leader proved too much for us to bare. We struggled the whole year as we finished the season with a 14-16 record. A stark comparison of what we had expected. I do not recall much from that season as it was all lost in a nightmarish fog.

My senior campaign on the basketball team was better as I was chosen co-captain of the team. My classmate and I were the only seniors on the team as we were elected to the leadership positions.

The team also consisted of five juniors and five sophomores. I had several memorable moments from my final year of high school basketball.

One game, I made a full court shot at the end of the first quarter. My team had the lead and we were holding the possession while running the clock down to get the last shot of the quarter. I threw the ball away as the other team stole my pass to my teammate. The player from the other team raced down the court as the time on the game clock was about to expire. I was following him closely behind when I noticed him look up at the game clock.

I looked at the clock as well to see there was five seconds left in the quarter. He must have not seen the amount of time left on the clock as he hurled up a shot from just over the half court line. The shot missed badly as the rebound crashed off the backboard which bounced all the way out beyond the free throw line. I was there to gather the rebound in with one hand as I pivoted around quickly.

I knew that the buzzer could sound at any second since I had peeked at the clock on my way down the court. I heaved the basketball down court like a quarterback throwing a deep pass to a receiver downfield. I could tell that the shot was right on line the second that the ball left my hand. After the ball travelled about halfway to the goal, I heard the buzzer go off. A split second later the basketball rattled in the rim falling through the net.

The whole crowd erupted in cheer as the shot fell through the goal. The noise from the crowd was so loud that it hurt my ears. I felt the decibels from the loud eruption going through my body. I thought that I was going to pass out there for a moment as a strange feeling came across me. My whole team rushed the court jumping all over me as they reacted in jubilation.

My best game of the year was against our rival. The first game played in their newly dedicated gymnasium was against my team. They had not beaten my high school since 1968. They were out for blood that night as they chanted in their locker room before the game. My team could hear them through the wall. We just set there staring into space focused on the task at hand.

Our coach was out in the hallway and heard their team chanting loudly, and he rushed into our locker room to check on us. He looked around at us to see that we were focused and unaffected by their hoopla. He never said a word as he just turned around and left the locker room. It felt like I was walking on air that night as I witnessed my teammates walking on air too.

They were all gliding down the court with ease as they appeared to be light on their feet. We won the game by twenty points as I lead the team with a triple double performance. I had 14 points, 15 assist, and 12 rebounds in the dominant annihilation of our rivals on their home court. I sat out most of the fourth quarter as our bench players sustained the big lead that we had built.

I had a great feeling that night as the game ended, and I walked off the court knowing that we were the best team. The stands were packed with fans from both teams which witnessed my outstanding performance. I wanted to impress all of them that night as I completed my agenda with flying colors. That game was the best team performance that I had ever witnessed.

Another memorable moment from my senior year of basketball happened after the game had ended. We had won the game as we were walking off of the court. A player from the other team was walking right in front of me when I noticed one of his teammates grab the basketball. He hurled the ball towards the goal in anger as the ball ricocheted off the backboard.

The basketball bounced out beyond the free throw line and bounced one time before smashing into the back of the head of his teammate. The impact of the ball against his head was so forceful that his head careened forward as the ball rung against his head. He turned slowly to look behind him to see who had hit him with the ball. I was the first person that he saw. He walked over to me with an angry look on his face, and I said to him, *"I didn't do it!* Then, he responded to me, *"Who the hell did then?"* I pointed over to his teammate that had thrown the ball and said, *"He did!"*

At that time, he looked over at his teammate to see him standing near the free throw line. His teammate just hung his head in shame as he drooped his arms and body as well. He knew from his teammates reaction that I was telling him the truth about the incident. He just turned around and walked off the court my teammates and I followed closely behind him.

My fellow senior and I lead the team to a 20-12 record my senior year while reaching the state regional tournament. We were the first team from my high school since 1958 to win a game in the state regional tournament. I was forced to play my final high school game with three broken ribs.

I was injured in the district tournament championship game when a player from the other team hit me in the ribs with his knee as he attempted to dunk the basketball. We won our first game in the state regional tournament before losing in the second round of the tournament.

During the game that we lost, our coach had called a timeout. We were in the huddle when all of my starting teammates were complaining about one of their players roughing them up. He had not bothered me up to that point as I had not even noticed him. I was trying to protect my rib injury so I was shying away from a lot of physical contact. They said, *"That 34 is playing dirty!"* Our coach turned to me and asked me if I had any trouble with him. I told him that I had not even noticed him.

We broke the huddle and returned to the court. I was watching their tough guy running down the court when he saw me looking at him. He yelled at me across the court saying, *"What the hell are you looking at?"* I just looked away at first because I was embarrassed that he had caught me looking at him. Suddenly, I felt a jolt of adrenaline shoot through my body as we were still running down the court.

We were near the half court line when I turned to him and said, *"A fucking pussy!"* He turned away from our stare down and ran off in the opposite direction from me. Not long after our encounter, we had another timeout. Our coach asked the guys if that 34 was still bothering them. Everyone of them was shaking their head and said, *"No, no, he has not bothered us one bit."* Our coach looked at me with an amazed look on his face before smiling at me.

He knew that I was playing with three broken ribs, but I would still take up for my teammates. We lost the game by a good margin as they were the better team. Their team went on to win the state regional tournament that year. The loss ended our season and my high school basketball career. A career that was never the same without my best friend on the court.

My high school graduation was approaching as the basketball season came to an end. I rode to school with one of my classmates one morning along with another friend from school. We smoked two joints on the way to school. My classmate had missed school the day before so he had to stop by the office for an absentee slip.

His eyes were very red as we walked down the school hallway. I advised him not to stop by the office because his eyes were so red. He just strutted off as he turned toward the office and said, *"I got this man!"* I went on to class and took my seat in my desk. I was surprised to see him enter the classroom a few minutes later as he strutted to his desk. Class had gone on for a few minutes as I thought to myself that he was going to get away with it.

All of a sudden, there was a knock on the door. It was the principal and the superintendent of the high school. They asked the teacher to speak with my friend that I had ridden to school with. I looked across the room to see his eyes as big as half a dollar as he exited the classroom. I made a hand gesture to him on his way out to not mention me, and he gave me a thumbs up as he left the room.

Not long after he had left the classroom, my classmates handed me a piece of bubble gum. They told me that I needed it for my breath. They told me that I was reeking from the marijuana. Then, they passed some Visine over to me. I told them that I had already used Visine out in the car, and I did not need any of it. They quickly told me that my eyes were extremely red, and I needed to put some of the Visine in my eyes.

About that time, our teacher said, *"Jim, come up to my desk."* I heard a gasp come over the classroom as I thought she was gonna send me to the office. I thought that she had seen my classmates helping me, and my classmates were afraid of the same thing that I was thinking. I approached her desk where she was sitting when she reached down to her left and slid a drawer open.

I saw her look in her purse for something as I stood there in front of the class. She pulled out a bottle of perfume from her purse and sprayed me three or four times. Then she instructed me to turn around as she sprayed my backside another three or four times. She put the perfume back in her purse and closed the drawer.

She told me to return to my desk as my classmates watched in amazement. My friend was not so lucky as the administration and the police searched his vehicle. They found the two joints that we had smoked that morning. We threw them in the ashtray as we pulled into the school parking lot. The joints were still smoldering when they searched his car. When they opened his car door smoke came barreling out of the car.

The principal said to him, *"Hell. I can get high just standing next to your car!"* He was not arrested for possessing the marijuana, but he was suspended from school for the rest of the year. It was his senior year as this proved to be a major setback for my friend, but he did keep his word to me by telling the administration that he had driven to school alone.

I was extremely nervous the whole first period, but I managed to elude any troubles. In second period, the principal called over the intercom for me to come to the office. I was scared as I made my way down the hall not knowing what might may be laying ahead. I thought that they would question me about my friend's incident.

The principal wanted to know how I got to school that morning. He said, *"How did you get to school this morning? I noticed that your car was not in the parking lot!"* I told him that I had ridden with another classmate of mine. He looked at me with disbelief as he said, *"O.K. Then, go back to class."* I was so worried that he would call that certain friend of mine to the office in order to validate my claim.

I approached that same friend in the hall between classes and asked him, *"Have they called you to the office?"* He replied, *"No. They have not. Why?"* I asked him, *"If they do call you to the office. Tell them that I rode to school with you."* He said, *"O.K. I will. I will give you a ride home too."* I thanked him for the kind deed and accepted his offer to take me home since my other friend had been dismissed from the premises.

The very next period between classes, he approached me in the hallway. He said, *"Man. What is going on? They called me in the office and questioned me about who rode to school with me. I told them that I had gone by your house and picked you up before school, and I was taking you home after school too."* I informed him about my other friend's incident as he was unaware of the news. The help from good friends that day saved me from certain disasters as God watched over me once again.

Another moment from my senior year, I was leaving school one day with a car load of pothead buddies when I decided to show off. I pushed the accelerator to the floor which threw gravel all over the place as we exited the parking lot. The next morning at school, the principal called over the intercom for me to come to the office.

He informed me that I had slung gravel all over him the day before as he was crossing the parking lot. He thought that it was done on purpose because he was standing right behind my car. He said that he was covered with bruises from the pelting of gravel that was thrown onto him. I told the principal that I had never even seen him that day. I was just showing off for attention. He told me to be more careful on the school grounds before dismissing me back to class.

A few days later, I was leaving school again with the same pothead buddies as I decided to show off once again. I waited until I was on the paved road in front of the gymnasium before romping the gas pedal to the floor. The tires spun and squealed as I speed down the road in front of the gymnasium. This time, I did see the principal standing out in front of the gym with some important looking people wearing suits.

He shook his head as I roared past him and the visitors. The principal called me to the office again the next morning at school. He said, *"First, you pelt me with gravel showing off like an idiot! Then, you go ripping by the gym squalling your tires and revving your engine on school grounds again! After, I had just spoken to you! If you want to drive like an idiot at least wait until you are off of the school grounds!"* I apologized for my behavior as he sent me back to class.

Another time, I was leaving school again with the same buddies as I showed off for the third time. I waited until I was around the front of the high school when I pushed the accelerator to the floor. I raced by the front of the school when I noticed the principal taking down the flag from the flagpole. He shook his head again as he noticed that it was me driving by at a very high rate of speed.

Again, I was called to the office by the principal the very next day. He said, *"What is your problem? You could have killed somebody flying by the school like that! Parents are picking up their children, and there you are driving recklessly! If you are going to drive like an imbecile at least wait until you are up on the highway! Do not drive that way ever again! Anywhere near the school! This is your last warning!"*

He dismissed me back to class once again with that final warning. I realized how dangerous it was because of all the children in the area. I never showed off again on the school grounds after that third encounter. I was just a thrill seeker that never meant no harm, but I did appreciate the many chances the school had offered to me. Again, God was watching out for me by keeping me out of trouble.

My most embarrassing moment from my senior year of high school occurred one morning when I skipped the first two periods of class. My pothead buddies and I had been riding around and smoking pot for two hours while everybody else was at school. I noticed a school bus parked in front of the high school upon our arrival. I said, *"I wonder what that bus is doing parked out front?"*

One of my buddies noticed that my mother's car was also parked out front too. They said, *"Ain't that your mom's car? I bet that is the who's who bus. They announced it on the intercom yesterday that they would be leaving this morning for picture day. Oh, yeah! You skipped school yesterday too!"* I was supposed to be on that bus as I had won several who's who awards, but I had forgotten all about it because I was too busy smoking pot.

I parked my car in the parking lot around the back of the school, and I quickly made my way into the high school. I was still stoned from the morning smoke fest as I approached my mother and the principal waiting in the hall. They said to me, *"Where the hell have you been? The bus has been filled with the who's who winners, and they have been waiting on you for two hours! And the photographer is waiting too."*

My mother was ashamed and embarrassed by my behavior. As she was still wearing her robe from the early morning phone call. My principal told me that I was going to receive a paddling, but we needed to get going in order to take the who's who pictures. My mother departed the high school as the principal decided to paddle me upon our return from the picture day.

I told the principal that they should have left without me, and he told me that they could not leave me because I had won the most categories of anyone. He told me to go and get on the bus with rest of the students. That was like stepping into a hornet's nest. Everybody on the bus was very angry and disappointed with my irresponsibility. They scolded me with a thrashing of slurs that were relentlessly thrown my way. Some of the girls were crying because their makeup had to be retouched from the excessive heat while they were waiting for me.

Everybody else was dressed in the best clothes as they had planned for the event for months. They asked me, *"Where have you been? What is your excuse? I got to hear his one!"* I told them that I had forgotten about the annual event. They replied, *"He forgot! He forgot! How could he forget! I have had this day circled on my calendar for months now!"*

I told them that I had other things going on and there was more to life than who's who pictures. They said, *"Yeah, like what? Riding around and smoking pot with your loser friends!"* I turned around to yell at them, but the principal ripped into me as well. He said, *"Don't you say a word to them! They have every right to be angry with you! You let all of us down!"*

I was wearing a sleeveless t-shirt because I had P.E. for the third period, and I was not anticipating taking any pictures. My classmate was wearing a sweater with a button-up shirt underneath. So, he let me wear his sweater for the pictures. I heard the girls saying, *"Look what he is wearing! I am not taking a picture with him wearing that t-shirt!"*

My friend saved the day for us by lending his sweater to me. He said, *"My mom is going to be mad because that is her favorite sweater."* I apologized to all of them to no avail as they were all still angry at me upon our return to the school. The principal lead me straight into the office as soon as we walked in the front door of the high school.

He gave me three licks with a paddle and scolded me for my bad decisions. I never meant to let any of them down because they were all important to me, but I had simply lost track of time and forgotten all about the event. I was looking forward to that day because I could miss school without getting into any trouble. I was mad at myself for such a blunder.

I had missed so many days during my senior year of high school that I had to stay two extra weeks. The days that I had skipped school coupled with my sick days accumulated to over forty days. The principal called me into his office to discuss the matter. He informed me that I would have to stay until the very last day of school in order to make-up for some of the missed days.

The rest of the seniors were set to graduate on May 15 as they would not return to school beyond that date. I would have to continue until May 29 when the school year officially ended. They allowed me to participate in the graduation ceremony, but I did not receive my diploma that night as the case was empty.

I went to school everyday for those two weeks with all of my fellow classmates no longer there. The underclassmen and younger students from the elementary school were still attending classes along with me. The principal made me wait as long as he could before giving the diploma to me.

My last day of high school the halls were empty. All of the other students were not required to be present that day. Even the elementary students were not present. I waited around until after lunch, and I went to the principal's office to inquire about my diploma. I told him, *"When am I going to get my diploma? All of the other students are gone! I even saw the kindergarten children leaving already!"*

He told me to go back to the library, and he would call me after a while. He said, *"It is not my fault that you skipped school all those days! You are lucky to be getting a diploma at all!"* About an hour or two later, the principal finally called for me to come to the office.

He was standing at his desk holding the document in his hand. He reached out his hand to give me the diploma and said to me, *"Have a nice life. I wish you all the best. You have certainly been an unforgettable student. Both good and bad."*

CHAPTER 9
GENUINE LOVE

My years in school were filled with many ups and downs, but through it all God always looked after me. Blessing me with many good friends and good times. The people from my school and community were some of the finest people that I have ever had the pleasure to meet. They were patient and understanding with me as I made my way through life.

They lived and loved with a genuine perspective that focused on good morals and virtues. They valued family, friends, community, and God. We lived in an era that signified an end to the old ways of life all while creating the launch of a new technological age. A time of rotary telephones, pay phones, typewriters, adding machines, and public broadcast television.

We did not have computers, the internet, home video games, cell phones, or cable television for many years, but the technological advances from that generation produced some of the earliest versions of many innovative inventions. Those days were more about close personal relationships which required eye contact and a firm handshake. An era where ones word was worth the price of gold.

A close knit community where families knew families while showing each other love and support. An age with very few violent crimes committed because of the loyalty and vigilance which was demonstrated within the community on a daily basis. A town where everybody knew each other, and they acknowledged one another with a smile and a wave.

They would greet each other by saying, *"How are you doing?"* Then with a simple reply, *"I am doing fine. How are you?"* Furthermore acknowledging, *"I am doing fine too. Thank you for asking."* I thank God everyday that I was blessed with the people in my life. We formed bonds that would last a lifetime, and our love for one another which would last an eternity.

The traditional, old fashioned approach which seems to be fading away into the past. A time gone by that I relish with all of my heart. A little piece of heaven right here on Earth. I hope that our future generations can learn from our proper predecessors and demonstrate their techniques that were passed down to them from the greatest generation of American history. A life filled with love, virtues, togeth- erness, and God is a blessed life that could be well within reach for each of us to obtain.